D1001747

THE CONDITIONS OF AGRICULTURAL GROWTH

THE CONDITIONS OF
AGRICULTURAL GROWTH

*The Economics of Agrarian Change
under Population Pressure*

BY

ESTER BOSERUP

With a Foreword by
NICHOLAS KALDOR

ALDINE PUBLISHING COMPANY
CHICAGO

FIRST PUBLISHED IN 1965

This book is Copyright under the Berne Convention. All rights reserved. Apart from any fair dealing for the purpose of private study, research, criticism or review, as permitted under the Copyright Act, 1956, no part of this publication may be reproduced, stored in a retrieval system or transmitted, in any form or by any means, electronic, electric, chemical, mechanical, optical, photocopying, recording or otherwise, without the prior permission of the copyright owner. Enquiries should be addressed to the Publishers.

© *George Allen & Unwin Ltd*, 1965

Second printing, 1966
Third printing, 1969
Fourth printing, 1970
Fifth printing, 1972
Sixth printing, 1973
Seventh printing, 1974
Eighth printing, 1975
Ninth printing, 1977

Published in the United States of America By
Aldine Publishing Company
529 South Wabash Avenue
Chicago, Illinois 60605
ISBN 0-202-07003-4
Library of Congress Catalog Number 65-19513

Printed in the United States of America

FOREWORD

It is a great pleasure for me to introduce Ester Boserup to English readers. I first knew her when she joined the Research and Planning division of the Economic Commission for Europe in Geneva in 1947 of which I was then the Director. I soon discovered that she was one of the ablest and most imaginative members of our group, and her work contributed greatly to the early success of the annual Economic Surveys. Her ingenuity in using statistics to exhibit the trends in world trade, and to pin-point the causes of the disequilibrium between the dollar and the non-dollar world, deserves public recognition.

Since that time, Mrs Boserup has had an interesting and varied career, which included working in India and other Asian countries for some years under Professor Myrdal in a study of Asian agriculture, the results of which are yet to be published.

Her present work clearly reflects her experience in Asia. It analyses the problem of agricultural progress in primitive communities from an entirely new angle: she regards the growth of population as the autonomous factor making for a steady intensification in agriculture, which in turn brings a whole host of economic and sociological changes in its train. Her main thesis is that, contrary to the prevailing view, primitive communities with a sustained population growth have a better chance of getting into a process of genuine economic development than primitive communities with stagnant or declining populations. As she herself emphasizes however, this thesis is subject to qualifications: it may not be true of communities with a very high rate of population growth which are already densely peopled, and which are unable to undertake the investment necessary for introducing still more intensive methods of agricultural cultivation.

The main impression, however, that will strike the reader of this book is that primitive agricultural communities are 'dynamic'. They are subject to continuing change in agricultural technology, induced by population pressure; even though these changes may not be as fast or dramatic as those experienced recently in the agricultural sectors of industrially advanced countries. Whether one fully accepts her thesis or not, I am certain that her original approach to one of the most important problems of our age is bound to be extremely fruitful in stimulating further thought.

King's College, Cambridge   NICHOLAS KALDOR

CONTENTS

INTRODUCTION

Ever since economists have taken an interest in the secular trends of human societies, they have had to face the problem of the interrelationship between population growth and food production. There are two fundamentally different ways of approaching this problem. On the one hand, we may want to know how changes in agricultural conditions affect the demographic situation. And, conversely, one may inquire about the effects of population change upon agriculture.

To ask the first of these two questions is to adopt the approach of Malthus and his more or less faithful followers. Their reasoning is based upon the belief that the supply of food for the human race is inherently inelastic, and that this lack of elasticity is the main factor governing the rate of population growth. Thus, population growth is seen as the dependent variable, determined by preceding changes in agricultural productivity which, in their turn, are explained as the result of extraneous factors, such as the fortuitous factor of technical invention and imitation. In other words, for those who view the relationship between agriculture and population in this essentially Malthusian perspective there is at any given time in any given community a warranted rate of population increase with which the actual growth of population tends to conform.

The approach of the present study is the opposite one. It is based throughout upon the assumption—which the author believes to be the more realistic and fruitful one—that the main line of causation is in the opposite direction: population growth is here regarded as the independent variable which in its turn is a major factor determining agricultural developments.

Actual events in the present period should go some way to make this change of perspective acceptable. Few observers would like to suggest that the tremendous increase in rates of population growth witnessed throughout the underdeveloped world in the two post-war decades could be explained as the result of changes in the conditions for food production. It is reasonably clear that the population explosion is a change in basic conditions which must be regarded as autonomous, in the sense that the explanation is to be sought, not in improved conditions of food production, but in medical invention and some other factors which the student of agricultural development would regard as independent variables.

The burden of the present study is, then, to show that this line of causation, where agricultural developments are caused by population trends rather than the other way round, is the dominant one, not only in the special and obvious case of the two decades since 1945, but in agricultural development generally. The author hopes to have shown that this approach is conducive to a fuller understanding of the actual historical course of agriculture, including the development of patterns and techniques of cultivation as well as the social structures of agrarian communities.

The fact that attention was mainly focused on food production as a limiting factor for population growth—in accordance with Malthus' main doctrine—did not prevent economists also paying attention to the question of how population growth, in its turn, affects agricultural production. Indeed, the theory of rent as developed by the classical economists was one part of the answer to this question: what happens to food production when population increases? However, the particular way in which this problem was tackled by the classical economists was determined by somewhat special conditions for agriculture in the Western Hemisphere in their time and this resulted in an over-simplified account of the changes in agricultural patterns that are brought about by the pressure of population growth. This point is of crucial importance for everything that follows in the present study, and some further explanation must be offered already at this stage.

The classical economists were writing at a time when the almost empty lands of the Western Hemisphere were gradually taken under cultivation by European settlers, and it was therefore natural that they should stress the importance of the reserves of virgin land and make a sharp distinction between two different ways to raise agricultural output: the expansion of production at the so-called extensive margin, by the creation of new fields, and the expansion of production by more intensive cultivation of existing fields.

This over-simplified conception of agricultural expansion has lingered on in economic literature, and even today it is this type of analysis that is usually offered when problems of underdeveloped countries are discussed. Why this approach is unsuitable for a general theory of agricultural development is most easily understood if it is remembered that many types of primitive agriculture make no use of permanent fields, but shift cultivation from plot to plot. This fact, which seems to have been ignored by classical economists, is fundamental for our problem, for it follows from it that in primitive types of agriculture there is no sharp distinction between cultivated and uncultivated land, and that it is impossible, likewise, to distinguish clearly between the creation of new fields and the change of methods in existing fields.

This study attempts to draw the full conclusion from this insight. The very distinction between fields and uncultivated land is discarded and instead emphasis is placed on the frequency with which the land is cropped. In other words, it is suggested that we consider a continuum of types of land use ranging from the extreme case of truly virgin land, i.e. land which is never cropped, through land cropped at shorter and shorter intervals, to that part of the territory in which a crop is sown as soon as the previous one has been harvested. It is the intention by this new approach to provide the framework for a dynamic analysis embracing all types of primitive agriculture, those which proceed by cropping a plot a single time after which it is left fallow for a generation or more, as well as types of agriculture with continuous cropping of virtually the whole area several times a year.

Once the time-honoured distinction between cultivated and uncultivated land is replaced by the concept of frequency of cropping, the economic theory of agricultural development becomes compatible with the theories of changing landscape propounded by natural scientists. The fathers of the traditional economic theory—in agreement with the natural scientists of their own time—regarded as immutable natural conditions many features which scientists now consider to be man-made and, in particular, the distinction between naturally fertile land and less fertile land was considered a crucial element in the explanation of agricultural change.

By contrast, when the analysis is based upon the concept of frequency of cropping, there can be no temptation to regard soil fertility exclusively as a gift of nature, bestowed upon certain lands once and for all. Thus, soil fertility, instead of being treated as an exogenous or even unchangeable 'initial condition' of the analysis, takes its place as a variable, closely associated with changes in population density and related changes in agricultural methods.

One of the disadvantages of the usual type of analysis is that it leads to a one-sided conception of the agricultural enterprise. Attention is likely to be focused upon what happens in the cultivated field, as distinguished from the whole group of activities that are needed in a given system of agriculture. Undue importance is often attached to the number of times the fields are ploughed or weeded while the changes which take place in the area classified as 'uncultivated land' tend to be overlooked. When attention is instead focused on the frequency with which the different parts of the area belonging to a given holding, village or tribal area is cropped, an important fact springs to the eye: most or all of the land added to the sown area as population increases in a given territory was used already, as fallow land, pasture, hunting ground, or otherwise. It follows that when a given area of land comes to be cropped more frequently than before, the purposes for which it was hitherto used must be taken care of in a new way, and this may create additional activities for which new tools and other investment are required. Thus, the new approach to agricultural development which is signalled by the concept of frequency of cropping draws the attention to the effects upon agricultural technology which are likely to result from population changes. This is in sharp contrast to the usual approach which takes agricultural technology as a largely autonomous factor in relation to population changes.

It is an essential problem in the economics of population changes to find out how such changes are likely to affect investment and it is generally agreed that the degree of security of tenure for the cultivator is one of the important determinants of investment. One of the advantages of the concept of frequency of cropping, as suggested in the present study, is that it makes it possible to bring fallow land, pastures and animal husbandry within the purview of the analysis and thus to appreciate the close relationship between changes in technical and economic factors on one hand and changes in land tenure on the other. In short, this new approach enables us to treat land tenure as an endogenous factor, with the result that arbitrary or unrealistic assumptions about tenure can be avoided in the analysis of investment problems.

The neo-Malthusian school has resuscitated the old idea that population growth must be regarded as a variable dependent mainly on agricultural output. I have reached the conclusion, to be substantiated in the following chapters, that in many cases the output from a given area of land responds far more generously to an additional input of labour than assumed by neo-Malthusian authors. If this is true, the low rates of population growth found (until recently) in pre-industrial communities cannot be explained as the result of insufficient food supplies due to overpopulation, and we must leave more room for other factors in the explanation of demographic trends. It is outside the scope of the present study, however, to discuss these other factors—medical, biological, political, etc.—which may help to explain why the rate of growth of population in primitive communities was what it was. Throughout, our inquiry is concerned with the effects of population changes in pre-industrial societies on agriculture and not with the causes of these population changes.

CHAPTER 1

THE DYNAMICS OF LAND UTILIZATION

The intensity of land utilization varies widely throughout the world. In large regions of Africa and Latin America, and in some parts of Asia, the system of land use is very extensive, with one to two years' cultivation followed by a fallow period of at least twenty years. The other extreme is found in Egypt and parts of the Far East, where most of the land which bears crops does so at least twice every year. Between these extremes are intermediate intensities of land use, and it is often found that one part of a country is under highly intensive cultivation, another part under annual cropping and a third part under various more or less extensive fallow systems.

Any classification of the systems of land use with respect to the degree of intensity is necessarily arbitrary to some extent. In order to simplify the analysis in the following chapters I have chosen a grouping with only five types of land use. These are as follows, in order of increasing intensity:

(1) *Forest-fallow cultivation.* Under this system of land use, plots of land are cleared in the forests each year and sown or planted for a year or two, after which the land is left fallow for a number of years sufficient for the forest to regain the land. This means that the period of fallow must be at least some twenty to twenty-five years. The type of forest which grows up in territories which are regularly used for forest fallow is known as secondary forest, as distinguished from the primary or virgin forest, which was never cultivated or was left uncultivated for a century or more.

(2) *Bush-fallow cultivation.* Under this system the fallow is much shorter, usually somewhere between six and ten years. No true forest can grow up in so short a period, but the land left fallow is gradually covered with bush and sometimes also with small trees. The periods of uninterrupted cultivation under bush-fallow systems varies considerably. It may be as short as one to two years (similar to conditions under forest fallow) and it may be as long as the fallow period, i.e. six to eight years. Many authors do not distinguish between forest and bush fallow systems, but group them together

under the label of long-fallow cultivation, or shifting cultivation.

(3) *Short-fallow cultivation.* The fallow lasts one year or a couple of years only. In such a short fallow period, nothing but wild grasses can invade the fallow, before the cultivator returns to the same plot or field. The system could therefore also be described as grass-fallow cultivation, but the term short fallow is to be preferred since under certain conditions land may lay fallow for very long periods without being invaded by anything but wild grasses. It is important, therefore, to distinguish between grass areas used in long-fallow systems and grass areas used in short-fallow rotations.

(4) *Annual cropping.* This is usually not considered a fallow system, but may be classified as such, because the land is left uncultivated, usually for several months, between the harvest of one crop and the planting of the next. This group is meant to include systems of annual rotation, in which one or more of the successive crops are sown grass or other produced fodder.

(5) *Multi-cropping.* This is the most intensive system of land use, since the same plot bears two or more successive crops every year. The planting of a new crop must therefore take place shortly after the harvesting of the preceding one and the fallow period is short or even negligible.[1]

Under the pressure of increasing population, there has been a shift in recent decades from more extensive to more intensive systems of land use in virtually every part of the underdeveloped regions. In some parts of the world, cultivators under the forest-fallow system have been unable to find sufficient secondary forest. They have then had to re-cultivate areas not yet bearing fully grown forest. In this way, the forest has receded and been replaced by bush. Again, in regions of bush fallow the cultivators have changed to short-fallow systems or annual cropping and many short-fallow cultivators have changed to systems of annual cropping with or without irrigation. In the densely populated regions of the Far East, the growth of population during this century has caused a rapid spread of multi-cropping.

THE HISTORICAL SEQUENCE

Shortening of fallow is not a feature which is characteristic of the twentieth century only. Historical investigations have revealed that there was a gradual shortening of fallow in western Europe during and after the Middle Ages ending in the change to annual cropping in

---

[1] The planting within a short period of several crops in immediate succession on the same piece of land, followed by many years of fallow, is here regarded as a type of long-fallow cultivation, and not as a case of multi-cropping.

the second half of the eighteenth century. But the evidence of a process of gradual shortening of fallow in Europe is not limited to the period for which we have written sources. Archeological research has given indication of the existence of a system of agriculture based on forest fallow in the neolithic period in Europe.[1] By combining the results of archeological and historical research we get the picture of a successive change in Europe from neolithic forest fallow to systems of shifting cultivation on bush and grass land followed first by short-fallow systems and in recent centuries by annual cropping.

Our knowledge of agrarian history is much more fragmentary for other parts of the world than for Europe. However, pollen studies and other archeological research point to the world-wide use in the neolithic period of a system of cultivation of forest plots, probably very much resembling the type of cultivation that is now found in many primitive communities. This contrasts with an earlier theory, according to which intensive cultivation in river valleys would have preceded the cultivation of forest land. The older theory seems to have been based upon the view that forest land was too difficult to cope with for very primitive peoples. This, however, ignores the fact that not felling but fire was the method of clearing forest land, and it seems that experts in the field now tend to think that river shore cultivation may have been taken up by descendants of tribes who had lost the forest land they had cultivated owing to desiccation or exhaustion and ended by crowding along the rivers. The Sahara and other deserts close to regions of ancient river cultivation are being searched for evidence to support or refute these theories.[2]

The historical sequence of the different types of cultivation is difficult to establish, because all the major agricultural systems used today—apart from modern chemical and mechanized agriculture—are several thousand years old. But it does not matter much for a discussion of the general process of development of agriculture, if some tribes may have discovered that the shores of a particular river could be sown and harvested annually without land preparation before or after forest-fallow cultivation had been used in the neighbourhood. Even if we cannot be sure that systems of extensive land use have preceded the intensive ones in every part of the world, there seems to be little reason to doubt that the typical sequence of develop-

[1] O. C. Stewart, 'Fire as the first Great Force employed by Man', in W. L. Thomas, jr. (ed.), *Man's Role in Changing the Face of the Earth* (Chicago, 1956), pp. 115–29; K. J. Narr, 'Early Food Producing Populations', ibid., pp. 134–47; H. C. Darby, 'The Clearing of the Woodland in Europe', ibid., pp. 183–210; J. Iversen, *The Influence of Prehistoric Man on Vegetation* (Copenhagen, 1949).

[2] R. O. Whyte, 'Evolution of Land Use in South-Western Asia', in L. Dudley Stamp (ed.), *A History of Land Use in Arid Regions* (UNESCO, Paris, 1961), pp. 57–114, and other articles in that publication.

ment of agriculture has been a gradual change—more rapid in some regions than in others—from extensive to intensive types of land use. The classification of types of land use suggested above is therefore more than just an attempt to identify and classify various types of agriculture existing today and in the past. It is supposed, at the same time, broadly to describe the main stages of the actual evolution of primitive agriculture, during prehistoric times and in the more recent past.

LAND USE IN THE TROPICS

In previous centuries, the European settlers and colonial officers in regions where long-fallow cultivation dominates were overlooking that the apparently unused forest and bush lands served as fallow for the native population. Large amounts of such land were expropriated for the use of European settlers or plantation companies or they were declared restricted forests where natives were not allowed to clear plots for cultivation. It was assumed that no damage was inflicted on the native population, as long as they were left in the possession of the land they had under actual cultivation and were given, in addition, a certain amount of uncultivated land. The latter was meant as an area for the collection of fuel and other materials and for the expansion of cultivation in case the population should increase.

This kind of land policy ignored the fact that large parts of the territories from which the natives were thus excluded had formerly served as fallow in long-fallow rotations. The expropriation of such land would necessarily compel the cultivators to shorten the fallow period and sometimes the soil became exhausted by excessive cultivation. The exhaustion of the soil in the native reserves and the complaints of the natives eventually opened the eyes of many Europeans to the existence of the systems of long-fallow cultivation and these have since been the subject of studies by many economists, agronomists and social anthropologists.

Most of the regions where long-fallow cultivation dominates today are found in the tropics, and this can largely explain why the long-fallow systems were considered to represent an adaptation to the special conditions of soil and climate in the tropical zone. We have an example of this line of thought in Pierre Gourou's widely read book *The Tropical World*.[1] He assumes in fact that the soil in most of the tropical zone cannot be used for other systems of cultivation than long fallow. In his view, only volcanic soil or soil regularly receiving

[1] P. Gourou, *Les pays tropicaux* (Paris, 1947; English revised edition, London, 1954).

top soil from other regions—by flooding or in other ways—would be able to support more intensive cultivation. This pessimism regarding the fertility of tropical land goes hand in hand with a Malthusian interpretation of the demographic situation in the tropics. Professor Gourou supposes that most of the tropics is sparsely populated because the land is unable to support cultivation for more than one year out of twenty and therefore unable to support a numerous population. Gourou's conclusion is that the number of people in the tropics has grown to what the territory can carry, and that additional population must largely be accommodated by means of industrialization and reliance on foreign trade.

The belief that there is little scope for intensive land use in the tropics was not left uncontested. It was discussed at the Inter-African Soil Conference in Leopoldville in 1955.[1] Both at this conference and in recent contributions by many experts and even by Gourou himself a considerably more optimistic view is taken concerning the scope for spreading methods of intensive land utilization in Africa and other tropical regions.[2] It is stressed that the land used for intensive cultivation, for instance in parts of Nigeria, is of the same type as that used in long-fallow rotations in Nigeria and elsewhere with similar climatic conditions. Fertility may be the result of the use of intensive methods of land utilization and not *vice versa*.

THE CHANGING LANDSCAPE

The discovery of the earlier existence of long-fallow systems in regions which are now either deserted or cultivated in intensive

---

[1] *Comptes rendus, 2ᵉ conférence interafricaine des sols, Leopoldville* (Brussels, 1955). See the paper presented by H. Vine, 'Is the Lack of Fertility of Tropical African Soils Exaggerated?', ibid., pp. 389–406.

[2] In an article published in 1962 Gourou says as follows: 'Enfin, on a trop dit que les sols tropicaux étaient d'une utilisation délicate . . . il est aujourd'hui permis de penser que l'Afrique ne manque pas d'étendues cultivables; elle récolte effectivement chaque année trois pour cent de sa surface totale alors que sa surface cultivable est au moins de cinquante pour cent de la surface totale.' P. Gourou, 'Les conditions du développement de l'Afrique tropicale', in *Genève-Afrique, Acta Africana*, vol. I, No. 1 (1962), pp. 49–50. *See also* P. Gourou, 'The Quality of Land Use of Tropical Cultivators', in W. L. Thomas, op. cit., pp. 336–46; A. T. Grove, 'Population Densities and Agriculture in Northern Nigeria', in Barbour and Prothero (ed.), *Essays on African Population* (London, 1961), pp. 115–36; K. M. Barbour, 'Population, Land and Water in Central Sudan', ibid., pp. 137–56; R. Dumont, *L'Afrique noire est mal partie* (Paris, 1962), p. 10; R. Morel, 'Les rotations et l'agriculture centrafricaine', and H. Laudelout, 'Fallowing Techniques of Tropical Soils', papers presented to the United Nations Conference on the Application of Science and Technology (Geneva, 1963), agenda item C.3.4.

systems of land use, has discredited the idea that the different fallow systems can be seen as adaptations to particular types of soil or climate. More and more authors seem to support a dynamic theory of land use, based on the recognition that there is a two-way connection between 'natural conditions' and fallow systems. It is now often suggested that in the neolithic period forests covered a much larger part of the land surface than now, and that the forest areas were reduced because they had been used in shifting cultivation and spoiled partly by too short fallow periods and partly by the use of fire for hunting purposes or because the fires used for land clearing got out of control. The forests would thus have been gradually replaced by bush and grass lands, in much the same way as that which can be observed nowadays in many regions of long-fallow cultivation and hunting.

When forests deteriorate, the grasses get their chance. In dense forest, grass cannot grow, but where the forest becomes thinner or is gradually replaced by bush wild grasses will spread. The grass-roots are not destroyed by fire, and land frequently exposed to fire therefore tends to become more and more grassy. The invasion of forest and bush by grass is most likely to happen when an increasing population of long-fallow cultivators cultivate the land with more and more frequent intervals. It has been observed, during the colonial period and after, that many areas previously under forest and bush gradually become savannah or other types of wild grass land, as a result of more or less frequent burning over or cultivation in relatively short rotations.[1] Many authors believe that a large share of the savannahs and other apparently natural grass lands owe their origin to similar changes in prehistoric times.

When forests are replaced by grass land natural fodder for cattle, horses and other herbivorous animals becomes available. Those who think that a large share of the grass lands of the world are man-made have therefore questioned the old theory, according to which the stage of nomadism would generally have preceded that of agriculture. According to that theory, nomadic tribes had first taken to clearing of land for cultivation when they had become too numerous to subsist by grazing of animals in natural grass lands. The sequence is now supposed to be the reverse: tribes which previously cultivated short-lived plots in forest and bush land have come to rely on the

---

[1] H. H. Bartlett, *Fire in Relation to Primitive Agriculture and Grazing, an Annotated Bibliography* (Michigan, 1957, multigraphed). This is a comprehensive collection of information about vegetational changes and related changes in land use. *See also* H. H. Bartlett, 'Fire, Primitive Agriculture and Grazing in the Tropics', in W. L. Thomas, op. cit., 692–712; and C. O. Sauer, 'The Agency of Man on the Earth', ibid., pp. 49–68.

grazing of animals only after they have cultivated forest plots for a very long period ending in the transformation of the forest into grass land.

Some authors are of the opinion that the retreat of the forests served to make the climate more dry and thus facilitated the spread of deserts. Others think that the spread of barren land is the result primarily of erosion caused by over-cultivation and by over-grazing by the herds of nomadic tribes. There is recent evidence from many parts of the world of over-stocked grazings being destroyed by over-grazing and wind erosion or by fires laying the land bare before the rainy season so that the top soil is carried away by water erosion. Barren hills deprived of their earlier vegetation and top soil abound in most regions of ancient civilization, from China to the countries on both sides of the Mediterranean. It is not unlikely that over-grazing in the past is mainly responsible for the present state of these areas.

It is a moot question, how much importance over-cultivation and over-grazing had in changing climate and increasing desert areas.[1] Dudley Stamp concludes a UNESCO study of land use in arid regions with this cautious summary of recent opinions: 'The rapid development of ecological studies has thrown doubt on the primeval character of much tropical vegetation. Whether any of the savannahs and tropical grass lands with scattered trees can still be regarded as climax vegetation, uninfluenced by man, becomes increasingly doubtful and the same is true of the "natural" vegetation of semi-arid and arid lands. If deserts are spreading it remains uncertain how far the spread reflects climatic change and how far the conscious or unconscious work of man.'[2]

The neo-Malthusians have not missed the chance to interprete the dynamic theory of land use as a confirmation of Malthusian beliefs. Malthus thought that the increase of population to a level beyond the carrying capacity of the land must lead to the elimination of the surplus population either by direct starvation or by other positive checks which in his opinion could be traced back to the insufficiency of food supplies as the basic cause. The new version of Malthusian theory is based on the idea that the increase of population leads to the destruction of the land; and that people, in order to avoid starvation, move to other land which is then destroyed in its turn. The neo-Malthusians collect all the evidence on the misuse of land and paint a picture of the world as a place where growing populations are pressing against a food potential which not only is incapable of increase

---

[1] Controversial ideas about this subject are expressed in the articles in op cit. and in L. Dudley Stamp, op. cit.

[2] Ibid., p. 379.

but is even gradually reduced by the action of these growing populations.

It is not to be denied that the food potential of the world has been narrowed down by populations, who did not know how to match their growing numbers by more intensive land use without spoiling the land for a time or forever. But nevertheless, the neo-Malthusian theories referred to above are misleading, because they tend to neglect the evidence we have of growing populations which managed to change their methods of production in such a way as to preserve and improve the fertility of their land. Many tribes did not become nomads destroying the land by their herds of herbivorous animals, but used these same animals to cultivate the grass lands in short-fallow rotations with the result that soil fertility was improved by animal manure. Others irrigated the dried-up lands and prevented erosion by terracing of the land. It is true that some regions which previously supported a more or less dense population are barren today, but it is equally true that regions which previously, under forest fallow, could support only a couple of families per square kilometre, today support hundreds of families by means of intensive cultivation. Growing populations may in the past have destroyed more land than they improved, but it makes little sense to project past trends into the future, since we know more and more about methods of land preservation and are able, by means of modern methods, to reclaim much land, which our ancestors have made sterile.

CHAPTER 2

THE INTERDEPENDENCE OF LAND USE AND TECHNICAL CHANGE

Before the systems of shifting agriculture had attracted the attention of economists, it seemed natural to take the chief tool of cultivation as the main criterion for the classification of systems of primitive agriculture. Accordingly, three broad types of agriculture were distinguished: (1) the most primitive one using neither hoe nor plough, (2) the hoe system, and (3) the plough system.

The digging stick is the most primitive of the main agricultural tools and the peoples who use digging sticks are the most primitive among the primitive agricultural tribes living today. By contrast, the highest levels of pre-industrial civilization have usually been reached by peoples with plough cultivation. It was natural, therefore, to view agricultural development as determined by a process of gradual change to better and better tools, whereby output per man-hour in food production was increased and part of the population made available for non-agricultural activities. One implication of this theory is that there is an antagonism between population increase and agricultural development in all primitive communities, since population growth makes it necessary to use less suitable land and thus gradually reduces output per man-hour. According to this view, the economic fortunes of any one people would seem to be directly related to its inventiveness or closeness to advanced civilizations and inversely related to its degree of proliferation.

This theory is apt to mislead because it ignores the fact that the kind of agricultural tool needed in a given context depends upon the system of land use: some technical changes can materialize only if the system of land use is modified at the same time, and some changes in land use can come about only if they are accompanied by the introduction of new tools.

In order to substantiate this point we must deal briefly with the tools and methods used together with the different systems of land use mentioned in the preceding chapter.

FALLOW SYSTEMS AND TYPES OF TECHNIQUES

The system of forest fallow is associated with a method of cultivation that varies little from one part of the world to another. On the plot chosen for cultivation the larger trees are felled with an axe or burned on the root after having been killed by ringing. Small vegetation is equally burned on the spot and logs and other unburned remnants of the natural vegetation are left in the field together with the ashes and the roots of trees and bush. Sowing and planting are done directly in the ashes without any land preparation and without the use of any other tool than perhaps a digging stick to scratch the ashes or punch the holes in which to plant the roots or sow the seed. It is not possible to use a plough on land cleared by this summary method.[1] Nor is it necessary since abundant ashes secure high yields, if soil and climate are reasonably favourable. The high yields last only a year or two. Hence, new plots are prepared each year and the old are left to grow forest after a single harvest or two.

After the burning of real forest the soil is loose and free of weeds and hoeing of the land is unnecessary. By contrast, when the period of fallow is shortened and, therefore, the natural vegetation before clearing is thin or grassy the land must be prepared with a hoe or similar instrument before the seeds or roots can be placed. Thus, the hoe is not introduced just as a technical perfection of the digging stick. It is introduced, typically, when an additional operation becomes necessary, i.e. when forest fallow is replaced by bush fallow.

The need for a further change of tool arises when the fallow, owing to too frequent cultivation, devastating fires or other reasons, gets still more grassy with less trees and bushes. The best method for the clearing of land under long fallow—the burning of the natural vegetation—is inefficient when the natural vegetation is grass. This is so, because the roots are left intact, and with many types of grasses these roots are exceedingly difficult to remove by means of hoeing. Thus, the use of a plough becomes indispensable at the same time as the gradual disappearance of roots of trees and bushes in the fallow

---

[1] 'The use of animal and plow in breaking the ground called for a clean surface. The planting stick and hoe may successfully work among the litter of a clearing where the trunks of fallen trees still obstruct the ground and the slash has been reduced by burning, but the plow achieves optimum results on permanently cleared ground. This, of course, refers to the plow in its final development. Lighter animal-drawn implements, like the *Hakenpflug* or the *Zoche*, served in slash and burn economy. But the exception will confirm the rule.' G. Pfeifer, 'The Quality of Peasant Living in Central Europe', in W. L. Thomas, op. cit., p. 250.

facilitates the use of a plough. Moreover, with the spread of grassy land in replacement of forests natural fodder for plough animals becomes available. Regions which change over from forest cover to grass are often invaded by nomads and herbivorous animals may thus appear in a region around the time when the local cultivators need them and become able to use them.

The need of a plough for short-fallow cultivation is so compelling that cultivators usually avoid the stage of short fallow if they are unable to use ploughs, owing to a lack of animals or for other reasons. Such cultivators prolong the periods of cultivation under bush fallow up to eight years or more instead of shortening the period of fallow. By re-cultivating the land year after year they avoid an excessive spreading of the wild grasses, and by keeping a relatively long fallow period when the cultivation periods are over, they give the bush a chance to cover the land and thus prevent its becoming too grassy. The result is the type of intensive bush fallow which can be observed for instance in many parts of Africa, where cultivation periods up to eight years alternate with fallow periods of similar length. If population becomes too dense for this type of cultivation, there is likely to be a transition directly to annual or multi-cropping. In this case the fallow period is not shortened but eliminated altogether.

When fallow is shortened or even eliminated in a given territory, some other method of preserving or regaining fertility must of course be introduced. There is thus a close association between the systems of fallow and the techniques for fertilization. Under forest fallow, the ashes left after the burning of the natural vegetation suffice to secure high yields. Under bush fallow, the amount of ashes is smaller and additional fertilization may be provided by burnt or unburnt leaves or other vegetable materials or turf brought to the cultivated plots from the surrounding bush land and mixed with the top soil by means of hoeing. Fertilization under short fallow is mainly or wholly provided by manure from the droppings of draught animals and other domestic animals and from human waste. Under still more intensive land utilization it is likely that several types of fertilization will be used simultaneously, including practices like green manuring, marling, composts, including household waste, silt from canals, etc.

Some of these methods of fertilization require no use of human labour, while others are highly labour intensive. Labour input per crop hectare is therefore likely to change as a result of changes in the length of fallow. Also the need for weeding is related to the fallow system. Weeding is unnecessary under forest fallow and rarely used under short fallow and bush fallow with a short period of cultivation. By contrast, weeding is indispensable under the intensive types of bush fallow mentioned above and in irrigated agriculture where the humidity during the growing season for the crops facilitates the spread of weeds.

Likewise, the use of irrigation techniques and other capital investment is related to the fallow system. Irrigation facilities and other land improvements, for instance terracing, are never used with long fallow and rarely with short fallow. But the introduction of multi-cropping often depends upon the creation of irrigation facilities and in dry regions the same may be true even of annual cropping. Short-fallow systems, on the other hand, may be practicable without irrigation even in very dry regions. Thus, the irrigation outfit is yet another kind of equipment which comes into use when the shortening of fallow makes additional operations necessary.

KIND OF TOOL *vs.* MAKE OF TOOL

The above description of the relationship between fallow systems on one hand and methods and tools on the other may suffice to show that systems of land use and agricultural techniques must not be treated as if they were independent of each other. Within a given fallow system, the range of choice with regard to the kind of tool and the input of labour and capital per crop hectare is rather narrowly circumscribed by technical considerations. Hence we cannot apply continuous production functions of the usual type when we wish to consider the effects of demographic changes in pre-industrial agriculture. This type of analysis would be appropriate only on the assumption that the additional labour provided by the increase of rural population could be utilized as a marginal addition to the input of labour in each existing field, by ploughing it more carefully or by weeding it better. But such an assumption would be unrealistic.

A growing rural population does not produce additional food by increasing the number of times the land is ploughed or by the weeding of fields under short-fallow cultivation which were hitherto left unweeded. Instead of such changes, which would not add much to total output, short-fallow cultivators are likely to take to annual cropping on a part of their land. This transition in its turn may call for the introduction of better ploughing, irrigation and weeding— or the shortening of fallow may have as its necessary concomitant the production of fodder crops for the animals. In other words, the additional labour is likely to be used as a means to undertake a radical change of the system of cultivation in part of the area, while no change is made in other parts of the area. With further increases of population more and more of the area may pass to the more intensive system of land use and production. Various aspects of this process of gradual change of land use and techniques will be discussed in Chapters 3 to 7.

However, not all kinds of technical change are linked to changes in fallow systems. A cultivator practising the system of forest fallow may use a stone axe, a crude iron axe made by the village blacksmith or a factory-made steel axe. For ploughs and irrigation equipment the choice is wider still, even if machinery operated by mechanical power is disregarded. Thus, the fact that there is a narrow range of choice for the *kind* of tool when the fallow system is given, does not exclude the possibility of a wide range of choice as between more or less efficient *makes* of one particular kind of tool. In fact, each system of cultivation can be practised with the help of very primitive or much more advanced makes of tool.

This distinction between the kind of tool (which is linked to the system of fallow) and the make of tool (which is unconnected with the system of fallow) leads us to consider three basic types of agricultural change:

(1) One kind of change is that in which rural communities change over from one kind of tool to another, e.g. from digging stick to hoe or from hoe to plough, but continue to use primitive makes of these tools produced by the cultivator himself or by a village blacksmith.

(2) Another type of change is that where rural communities not only change over from one kind of tool to another, but also gradually change over from home-made tools to tools made by artisans or factories in towns.

(3) Thirdly, there is the case where rural communities change to better makes of tool, but without changing the kind of tool. We have an example of this type of change in many tribal communities in Indonesia which have fairly recently replaced stone axes by factory-made axes, but continue to apply forest-fallow cultivation without either hoe or plough. The economic problems of this type of community will be discussed in Chapter 8.

CHAPTER 3

LABOUR PRODUCTIVITY UNDER LONG-FALLOW AND SHORT-FALLOW SYSTEMS

The reasoning in the two preceding chapters was based upon the assumption that the transition to more intensive systems of land use took place in response to the increase of population within a given area. This assumption is valid only if the intensive systems of land use either require so large capital investments that they are unlikely to be introduced before increase of population makes it necessary or profitable, or if they yield lower output per man-hour than the more extensive systems. On the other hand, if output per man-hour can be raised significantly with little or no capital investment, by the mere change to a more labour-intensive system of land use, we would expect such intensification to take place whenever the cultivators became aware of the existence of the intensive techniques, quite regardless of whether the density of population is high or low and whether population is stagnant or increasing. It is important, therefore, to ask in what way output per man-hour is likely to be affected by changes in systems of land use.

There is no *a priori* answer to this question. As mentioned above, the change from one fallow system to another is usually part of a more complex pattern of change involving also a change of factor proportions and a change of tools and methods. We must look for empirical evidence, especially by comparing differential crop yields in two systems of land use with differences in the input of labour and capital per unit of land in the same systems.

Of course we must not expect to get a conclusive answer to our question. Quantitative indications about output per man-hour in primitive agriculture are found in a few anthropological studies, farm management surveys and other sources. But the differences in output per man-hour emerging from these studies are only very partly to be explained by differences in fallow systems and methods; to a large extent they reflect differences in soil, climate, make of tool and quality of the human and animal labour used in the cultivation. We are very far from having sufficient material to be able to gauge the relative importance of each of these factors, but the available information nevertheless lends some support to common sense reasoning and may help us to arrive at some broad and tentative conclusions.

The question we must ask is this: Must output per man-hour—for a given population in a given territory—be expected to rise or to fall, in the relatively short run, when there is a shortening of fallow accompanied by the related changes in kind of tool and methods. By posing the question in this way we eliminate the disturbing influence of geographical variations in both natural and human factors and eliminate long-term effects, which cannot be expected to influence the choice at a given moment.

We must also eliminate the effect of differences in the make of tool. This problem is less complicated than it may seem at first glance, because a group of cultivators faced with an actual choice between various types of cultivation would in the normal case either have access to modern tools of all kinds or have to use primitive makes of all tools. In real life the choice will never be between forest fallow with stone axes and plough culture with factory-made ploughs.

FROM FOREST FALLOW TO BUSH FALLOW

The cultivators who subsist by the system of forest fallow are much more primitive in their whole way of life than cultivators who apply intensive methods of production. Moreover, there is no land preparation before sowing and no other agricultural tools than axes and digging sticks. It is tempting, therefore, to conclude that output per man-hour must be particularly low under this system of cultivation. But it is not so in actual fact. As stressed above, the comparison of output per man-hour in two different systems must be made in such conditions that differences in the human factor can be eliminated from the comparison. Thus, if we compare the cultivation system of forest fallow used as a subsidiary occupation by people on much higher stages of civilization with the intensive systems of cultivation, which these or their neighbours apply, we find that the cultivation system of forest fallow is usually referred to as an 'easy system', yielding a good crop with little input of labour.

It is obvious that the clue to the problem of output per man-hour of forest-fallow cultivation lies in the clearing of land, since no labour is needed for land preparation, weeding and manuring or for the care of draught animals. The time used for clearing forest for one or two years' cultivation varies widely with differences in climate, type of vegetation and make of the axe, but the important point to note is that land clearing for shifting cultivation in forest is in any case a summary operation. The fire does most of the work and there is no need for the removal of roots, which is such a time-consuming task when land has to be cleared for the preparation of permanent fields. The time used for superficial clearing under the system of forest fallow therefore seems to be only a fraction—perhaps ten or twenty per cent—of the time needed for complete clearing.[1]

It takes much longer to hoe and weed one hectare than to clear one hectare superficially with axe and fire.[2] When shortening of fallow leads to the clearing of bush instead of secondary forest and hoeing and weeding become necessary, the latter operations add more to labour requirements per hectare than is saved by the fact that bush rather than secondary forest has to be cleared away. In addition, yields per hectare are likely to decline considerably. Hence, there is a strong presumption that the transition from the system of forest fallow to that of bush fallow will be accompanied by a decline in output per man-hour.

If cultivation under bush fallow is intensified, through a lengthening of the period of successive cultivation on a given plot, the area of land that has to be cleared annually will be far smaller than the area under crops. However, by the same token it becomes necessary to prepare the land very carefully, and the summary type of clearing must therefore be replaced by a much more complete clearing of the land. Thus, the amount of labour saved because less land has to be cleared each year is at least partially offset by the fact that more labour will be required for clearing work per hectare. In addition, very

---

[1] A detailed estimate of 230 man-days per hectare for all operations with complete clearing of real forest (as preparation for cocoa production) is available in C. Daryll Forde and R. Scott, *The Native Economies of Nigeria* (London, 1946), p. 92. Estimates of 150 and 200 man-days per hectare for complete clearing of eight-year-old bush are given in tables in *Report of a Survey of Problems of Mechanization of Native Agriculture in Tropical African Colonies*, Colonial Office (London, 1950), pp. 20 and 28. For more summary clearing in preparation of yam production in Ibadan an estimate of 50–60 man-days per hectare is suggested in Daryll Forde and Scott, op. cit., p. 91. An estimate of 25 man-days per hectare for summary clearing of forest for shifting cultivation in Brazil is mentioned in P. Gourou, 'The Tropical World', op. cit., p. 29. S. F. Nadel gives an example from Nigeria where collective teams of young men by 'very hectic work' managed to clear bush in a summary way for yam cultivation in what corresponded to less than twelve eight-hour man-days per hectare and another example where only six such days were needed. It is important to note, however, that they did not work a whole day, but only two and a half hours in the first case and one hour in the second case. S. F. Nadel, *A Black Byzantium* (London, 1942), p. 249.

[2] Labour requirements per hectare for different operations needed in intensive bush fallow are available for experimental stations and a few private farms in British colonies in Africa in Report of a Survey, op. cit. Many tables showing labour input in China with intensive hoe cultivation are available in J. Lossing Buck, *Land Utilization in China* (Shanghai, 1937), vol. III.

labour-intensive methods—for land preparation, manuring and weeding—must be used if crop yields are to be kept unchanged despite the longer periods of uninterrupted cultivation of the land.[1]

Economists who ignore the process of shortening of fallow periods usually assume that diminishing returns per man-hour become a major problem only when a relatively high degree of population density has been reached.[2] If the land that is added to the cultivated area when population is increasing is assumed to be virgin land, then it is not unreasonable to think that as long as only some 5 to 10 per cent of total area is under cultivation in a given year, the additional land brought under cultivation may be of the same type as the one used hitherto. On the other hand, if we consider that 5 per cent of total area is about the maximum that can be cultivated in a given year in territories where the cultivation system is that of forest fallow, then a very different conclusion imposes itself. For an increase of the area under cultivation in a given year, for instance from 5 per cent to 10 per cent of total area is likely to imply a shortening of the fallow period to about half its previous length. It seems unavoidable that crop yields should decline or that additional labour would have to be devoted to land preparation, fertilization, etc. In both cases, output per man hour must fall. The decline of output per man-hour will affect all cultivators and not be limited to the additional ones only, such as would be the case if the land taken into cultivation were virgin land.

Primitive tribes seem to be well aware of the fact that they obtain the best result of a given effort by clearing and cultivating secondary forest. Many observers of communities living by the systems of long fallow report that bush is never cleared as long as secondary forest is available. Sometimes cultivators even resort to the clearing of virgin forest—a far more arduous task than the clearing of secondary forest —rather than clear the bush.

[1] 'The amount of work required on a *ngasu* (a first-year cultivation including the clearing of forest and bush. E.B.) is, strange as it may seem, only a little greater than that required on a *fute* (repeated cultivation in a second season. E.B.). On the latter there is no felling of trees and no killing of trees by fire, but this makes only a small difference. Hoeing is approximately the same on both formations, as grass and scrub of a first year *fute* (i.e. a second-year cultivation. E.B.) has usually grown quite tall by the month of June and is often of thicker strand. Moreover, there is generally more weeding to be performed on the *fute* than on the *ngasu*.' P. de Schlippe, *Shifting Cultivation in Africa* (London, 1956), p. 121.

[2] 'While good land was abundant the traditional sector could absorb increased numbers without a fall in *per capita* income or unemployment. But as good land gave out, diminishing returns to labour on the land, under-employment and work-spreading devices appeared in the traditional sector.' Benjamin Higgins, 'Employment Implications of the Application of Science and Technology in Less Developed Areas', paper presented to the United Nations Conference, op. cit., agenda item B.4.

THE ADVENT OF PLOUGH CULTIVATION

Let us now turn from the comparison of different types of long fallow to a comparison between the output per man-hour of cultivation with long and short fallow respectively. It was explained in chapter 2 that ploughing of the land is a near-necessity under the system of short fallow. We therefore have to ask the question of how cultivation with primitive ploughs drawn by draught animals compares to cultivation by means of fire, axe and hoe. It is usually taken for granted that output per man-hour will rise considerably, when the plough is introduced in a given community as replacement for the methods pertaining to long fallow. This is a doubtful generalization, however, if the change is from real forest fallow with very summary clearing by fire to the type of short-fallow cultivation or annual cropping with primitive ploughs which is found in underdeveloped countries.

To operate a primitive plough is hard work, both for the peasant and for the animal; and in addition to the plough work proper the peasant must take care of the animals. Unless he keeps a large herd of domestic animals and uses much labour to collect their manure, prepare composts and spread it carefully in the fields, he is likely to obtain much lower crop yields per hectare under short-fallow systems or annual cropping than by cultivating the same land under the system of forest fallow.[1]

Moreover, the type of crops grown under forest fallow are usually different from what they are under short fallow. Under the system of forest fallow it is possible for a family which cultivates and consumes mainly root crops to produce the amount of basic food it needs from a very small area. However, root crops are unsuitable under the system of short fallow because under that system the plants will need to be protected against grassy weeds by hand weeding. When long fallow is replaced by short fallow, food consumption usually becomes concentrated on cereals which require a smaller input of labour, but also yield much less per hectare in terms of calories.[2] Thus, if one wishes to gauge the differences in labour input necessary to cover requirements of basic food under the

[1] The system of forest fallow was applied in the nineteenth century in some regions of Russia with crop yields per hectare about three times those of plough cultivation. See I. Manninen, *Die finnisch-ugrischen Völker* (Leipzig, 1932), pp. 274–5.

[2] 'One acre planted to yams can feed a family of five for one year, whereas the produce of African-grown cereals from one acre in usually insufficient to sustain two people on one acre for the same period.' Lord Hailey, *An African Survey* (London, 1957), p. 869.

systems of long and of short fallow, the comparison must be between two systems of subsistence agriculture, differing in many respects besides in the length of the period of fallow: on one hand there is the system of long fallow, where a relatively small area is cultivated by means of fire, while additional food is provided by hunting and food collection in the forests. On the other hand there is the system of short fallow, where a relatively large area is ploughed and sown to cereals while the use of fire is given up, because it is ineffective against the grass roots. Under this system, the peasant has the additional chore of taking care of draught animals. Besides being used as a source of draught power these are sometimes used also as a source of animal protein.

Of these two patterns of agriculture, I am convinced that the former one usually requires less hard human labour than the latter. One important reason for this is that the system of short fallow does not allow the use of fire, the most powerful weapon primitive man ever invented in his struggle with nature. It is a general experience that primitive—and less primitive—cultivators usually refuse to abandon the cultivation of forest plots by means of fire, when Government officials prohibit this type of cultivation in order to avoid forest fires and erosion. There are many examples of Government offers to supply ploughs and draught animals being turned down because the cultivators found it easier to continue with the system of forest fallow.[1]

It was mentioned that in a region covered by forest or dense bush it is unlikely that animals suitable for drawing a plough would be found. Both the lack of animals and the higher output per man-hour of forest cultivation compared to primitive plough cultivation prevent the introduction of the plough at this stage. But if it becomes necessary, because of increase of the population, to shorten the period of fallow, output per man-hour is likely to decline for all the cultivators until a point is reached where higher output per man-hour could

---

[1] 'Primitive agriculture is located in the woodlands. . . . The larger the trees, the easier the task. . . . It is curious that scholars, because they carried into their thinking the tidy fields of the European plowman and the felling of trees by ax, have so often thought that forest repelled agriculture and that open lands invited it.' C. O. Sauer, 'The Agency of Man on the Earth', in W. L. Thomas, op. cit., p. 56. Also historical evidence seems to support the conclusion that primitive cultivators prefer long-fallow cultivation in the forest to short-fallow cultivation of grasslands. It is mentioned elsewhere in the publication quoted above that not only the American prairies, but also the European steppes were brought under the plough only in the second quarter of the nineteenth century when the steel plough had been invented and was being manufactured on a relatively large scale. Thus, before industry generally had reached a fairly advanced stage and the steel plough had spread widely, forest land had everywhere been preferred to permanent grassland (J. T. Curtis, 'The Modification of Mid-Latitude Grasslands and Forests by Man', ibid., p. 731).

be obtained by the introduction of animal-drawn ploughs. At that stage the use of the plough may spread, provided that suitable draught animals are available and that sufficient natural grazing is available for them. Under such conditions the introduction of the plough is to be regarded as a means to prevent a fall in output per man-hour rather than a means to raise it.

No general rule can say just what degree of population density must be reached before the introduction of the plough will be helpful by increasing output per man-hour, or at least by preventing its decline. This critical level of density where conditions are ripe for the plough to be introduced, depends upon natural factors and upon the type of plough and other tools that happen to be available to the community in question. The relative advantage of the plough is greatest on flat land in cold and humid climates where it is comparatively difficult to clear land by fire. Under such conditions, the plough is likely to be introduced before the density of population has reached as high a level as would be required under other natural conditions.

CHAPTER 4

CARRYING CAPACITY OF LAND AND PRODUCTIVITY OF LABOUR UNDER INTENSIVE AGRICULTURE

We have now reached the point in our investigation of output per man-hour under different systems of land use where the problem of fodder supply for draught animals must be considered.

Rural communities subsisting by the long-fallow cultivation systems have no draught animals and the supply of animal food for human consumption usually comes from hunting and fishing or from smaller domestic animals and fowl, which find their feed mainly in forest or bush. The upper limit to the area under cultivation at one and the same time is here given by the need of fallowing for the sake of maintaining crop yields, rather than by the need to provide feed for domestic animals. With the transition to a system of short fallow in which draught animals are used a new situation is created. The limit to the area which can be cultivated in a given year is now determined by the necessity of setting aside large areas for grazing by draught animals which feed mainly or exclusively on natural vegetation.

In most parts of the world, the area an animal can till with a primitive plough is much smaller than the area needed to feed it on natural grazing. Hence, under short fallow the need to provide fodder for the draught animals means that one of three conditions must be fulfilled: a considerable part of the land must be left as permanent grazing; or the cultivation period must be considerably shorter than the fallow period during which the fields are left to grow wild grasses for the animals to feed on; or, finally, a part of the harvest from the cultivated fields must be given to the animals.

If the animals are fed almost exclusively with non-cultivated fodder, the area cultivated in a given year under systems of short fallow can rarely be more than one-third of the total territory and usually the maximum is much lower. Nevertheless, the maximum share of the territory that can be under cultivation in one and the same year is higher under short fallow than under forest and ordinary bush fallow, because the period of fallow is much shorter. It follows that the carrying capacity for human population may be very much increased by the change, in a given territory, from hoe cultivation with long fallow to short fallow with animal draught power.

However, intensive systems of bush fallow with up to eight years of uninterrupted cultivation, followed by a similar period of fallow, have a larger carrying capacity for human populations than short fallow with ploughing by animals. Where cultivation under long fallow has developed into this intensive type, it may be impossible to relieve population pressure by a change to short fallow with feeding of the draught animals on natural grazing. If population is increasing in communities of this type a change directly to annual cropping or multi-cropping imposes itself.[1] As regards the technique of cultivation, there may then be a choice between continued reliance on hoeing or ploughing with the help of draught animals. If the plough cultivation is chosen, it is necessary either to leave a considerable share of the total area as permanent grazings or to feed the animals mainly on fodder produced in the fields; in the latter case, the fodder needed for a given number of animals can of course be provided from a much smaller area.

FROM NATURAL GRAZING TO PRODUCED FODDER

When produced fodder enters into our comparisons of output per man-hour it becomes necessary to define output net of this fodder, while the hours of human labour needed to produce it must of course be included in total man-hours. With the transition to feeding with produced fodder, nature's free gifts—natural grazing and fodder found by animals in forest and bush—are replaced by fodder provided by additional human toil. It is possible that net output will hereby increase because the animals become capable of tilling the land more efficiently and their manure becomes more valuable. But it is most unlikely that this increase in net output would fully compensate for the additional input of human labour; this would happen only in cases where a severe fodder shortage had led to a deterioration of the livestock. Apart from such cases, a change from natural to produced fodder will reduce average output per man-hour.

Owing to the seasonal character of agriculture (a subject to be dealt with in the next chapter) a couple of hectares is often all that can be ploughed per animal. If a draught animal ploughing a few hectares must be fed on produced fodder all the year round, or most of it, the

---

[1] Some densely populated regions of Nigeria are in this position today.

peasant must see his work load increase considerably.[1] It is not surprising, therefore, to observe in communities living by the system of short fallow that cultivators hesitate to undertake change to produced fodder when fallow or other grazing areas are becoming scarce owing to an increase of population. Instead, cultivators are apt, in this situation, to limit the additional labour as much as possible by exposing their animals to half-starvation on overgrazed areas of stubble and natural grazing during the long periods of the year, when the animals are doing little or no work. Only in the short seasons of field work would the animals be given some of the cereals or other food crops cultivated in the fields in order to keep them in tolerable working condition.

In most of the Indian subcontinent as well as in North Africa population increase in this century has contributed to create a serious grazing shortage with overcrowding of animals on the remaining fallow lands and permanent grazings, and with consequent deterioration of the livestock. A similar grazing shortage developed in Europe in the centuries preceding the agricultural revolution. As is well known, this European shortage of grazing was eventually circumvented by a change from the system of short-fallow cultivation to one of annual cropping with fodder plants as a regular part of the rotation.

Some of the fodder crops introduced into the European fields during the agricultural revolution were leguminous crops. Previously cultivation of leguminous crops for human consumption had taken place on a small scale only. The introduction of this new element of fertilization, simultaneously with a rise in the supply of animal manure, helped to bring about a sharp increase in yields of the other crops in the rotation. Thus, during the period when fallow was reduced to some months per year, there was nevertheless a considerable increase in output per crop hectare.

With higher yields per crop hectare of the traditional crops and more frequent cropping of the arable area total output both of crops and of animal produce rose sharply; at the same time, of course, total input of labour in agriculture rose markedly. How did the net

[1] Farm management studies for a number of years are available for some districts in the Indian States of Bombay, Madhya Pradesh, Madras, Punjab, Uttar Pradesh and West Bengal. In some of the districts surveyed in these sample studies draught animals are fed mainly on produced fodder, while in others they are fed mainly on common grazings, and in the latter case the cost to the peasant of keeping draught animals is very much lower than in the former case. Where bullocks are fed on common grazings, the computed costs of bullock labour used for one crop may account for less than 10 per cent of the total costs of that crop. Where they are fed on produced fodder, the percentage sometimes exceeds 50 (*Studies in Economics of Farm Management*, Ministry of Food and Agriculture, New Delhi, 1958–62, *passim*).

output per man-hour react to these changes? Was the fertilizing property of the leguminous plants—their ability to bind nitrogen from the atmosphere—sufficient to offset the decline in average net output per man-hour caused by the change from natural to produced fodder for draught and other domestic animals? It seems most unlikely that this should have been the case.

The change in western Europe to annual cropping used to be described as the result of an autonomous technical revolution, namely the alleged discovery of the possibility of cropping the land without fallow by the use of crop rotations with fodder plants, of which some were leguminous. The rapid growth of population in western Europe was considered to be the result rather than the cause of this change. However, economic historians have revised the traditional explanation of the agricultural revolution. It has been revealed that virtually all of the methods introduced in this period had been known beforehand and that crop rotations without fallow and with leguminous crops were used in the ancient world in the Mediterranean as well as other regions.[1]

Some of the intensive practices introduced in the fields during the agricultural revolution in Europe had been in use in gardens, and were now extended to the fields; other methods seem to have disappeared from Europe for many centuries, but continued to be applied in other and more densely populated parts of the world. Their reappearance began in the densely peopled and highly urbanized valley of the Po, and from there they moved to England and northern France via densely peopled and highly urbanized Flanders where the turnip, for instance, was used already in the thirteenth century. These few facts suggest that the transition in Europe from short fallow to annual cropping was not the result of contemporary inventions; it could more plausibly be described as the spread of various methods of intensive cultivation most of which, although known since antiquity, was little used in Europe until the increase of urban population raised the demand for food and the increase of rural population provided the additional labour needed for a more intensive cultivation of the land in the most densely populated regions of the continent.

It is suggested, in other words, that for many centuries it had not been worthwhile for European cultivators to produce leguminous and other fodder crops, because the addition to total output, which

[1] Marc Bloch, *Les caractères originaux de l'histoire rurale française* (Paris, 1931), pp. 217–23; C. E. Stevens, 'Agriculture and Rural Life in the Later Roman Empire', in *The Cambridge Economic History* (Cambridge, 1942), vol. I, pp. 91–104; C. Parain, 'The Evolution of Agricultural Techniques', ibid., see especially pp. 131–2. *See also* R. O. Whyte, 'Evolution of Land Use in South-Western Asia', in L. Dudley Stamp, op. cit., p. 86.

they would make it possible to obtain, would have failed to compensate for the addition to total labour input, required for producing them and feeding them to animals. As long as sufficient natural fodder was available, the knowledge of the fertilizing effects of leguminous crops had thus been lying dormant and only later, when the increase of population in some regions of Europe raised the demand for livestock and other agricultural produce and caused a shortage of grazing, did the new pattern begin to assert itself. The technique of fertilization by means of leguminous fodder plants may thus be added to the list of agricultural techniques which comes in use only when a certain population density is reached.

FROM DRY TO IRRIGATED AGRICULTURE

When population density exceeds a certain level in a region where agriculture is based on ploughing with animals, a change to produced fodder in annual rotations is not the only alternative to a grazing shortage. Another solution is to discontinue the cultivation of the poorest land, hitherto used in rotations with short fallow, and leave it as permanent grazings, while the better land is cropped once every year or more with the use of labour-intensive techniques of fertilization and, if necessary, irrigation. This is the method usually applied in Asia, when the density of population exceeds a certain level.

Intensification of this Asian type not only increases the area that can be cropped in a given year. It may also raise yields per crop hectare, particularly in the cases where a transition from dry to irrigated agriculture is involved. However, these higher yields per crop hectare are obtained by a much higher labour input per crop hectare, even in cases where the water for irrigation is supplied from canals, built and operated by others than the peasant himself. Harvest work per crop hectare is roughly proportionate to yields, and irrigated crops must often be weeded by hand and sometimes transplanted. Total labour input per crop hectare of a given crop may be twice as high as for dry cultivation even where watering is by gravitation and requires very little labour.[1]

In cases of labour-intensive irrigation where water is lifted from rivers, tanks and wells and spread over the fields by means of human and animal labour, the work of watering alone may require more

[1] See the table on page 40, which reproduces figures for labour input with dry and irrigated crops in the same Indian villages. It should be noted in interpreting these figures that irrigation in the districts surveyed in Bombay and Madras is of the labour-intensive type (wells and tanks), while that of the districts in Punjab and Uttar Pradesh is of the capital-intensive type (canal irrigation).

human labour days than all the operations with a dry crop added together. Average output per man-hour seem usually to be lower with this type of irrigation than with dry cropping under similar circumstances. Chinese peasants applying irrigated agriculture sometimes obtain crop yields which are extremely high for cultivation without chemical fertilizers, but in such cases labour input per crop hectare may be up to six hundred working days per crop hectare for a crop of cereals.[1] This is ten to twenty times the usual labour input for dry

AVERAGE LABOUR DAYS PER HECTARE AND CROP IN INDIAN AND CHINESE AGRICULTURE

	Prep. Tillage	Sow-ing	Manur-ing	Inter-culture	Irriga-tion	Har-vesting	Thresh-ing	Total
WHEAT								
India, Bombay, dry	13	4	—	2	—	11	9	39
India, Bombay, irrigated	16	8	—	14	35	15	18	106
India, Madhya Pradesh, dry	21	5	1	3*	—	7	10	47
India, Punjab, dry	11	4	—	1	—	9	8	33
India, Punjab, irrigated	19	5	1	4	7	11	18	65
India, Uttar Pradesh, irrigated	27	5	—	1	8	20	24	85
China, North, dry	11	5	5	5	—	14	14	54
China, South, dry	26	13	18	27	—	27	31	142
SORGHUM								
India, Bombay, dry	7	2	—	4	—	7	5	25
India, Bombay, irrigated	11	3	—	24	13	15	11	77
India, Madras, dry	6	4	1	2	—	22	4	39
India, Madras, irrigated	13	7	4	8	44	30	4	111
China, dry	12	6	9	35	—	20	18	101
GRAM								
India, Bombay, dry	7	7	—	2	—	11	6	33
India, Bombay, irrigated	5	7	—	3	18	11	11	55

* Watching for birds only.

Sources: The figures for India are computed from tables in *Studies in Economics of Farm Management in Bombay in the Year 1956–7*, Ministry of Food and Agriculture (New Delhi, 1962) and corresponding volumes for Madhya Pradesh (1959), Madras (foreword dated 1960), Punjab (1962), and Uttar Pradesh (foreword dated 1960). The figures for China are computed from tables in J. Lossing Buck, *Land Utilization in China* (Shanghai, 1937), vol. 3.

crops of cereals in extensive plough cultivation of the type applied in underdeveloped countries.

Finally, it remains to consider output per man-hour in cases where more than one crop annually is taken from the same fields. Multi-cropping without irrigation seems in most cases to give lower average output per man-hour than annual cropping, because the additional crops are much more exposed to destruction due to excessive—or insufficient—amounts of water, or by the cold season, than the single annual crop which will normally be grown in the best growing season. Where irrigation is applied, both the need of heavy fertilization and the need of more watering for the crops grown outside the most suitable growing season reduce average output per man-hour below the level which could be obtained with a single crop in the same land. But there is a counterbalancing factor if multi-cropping allow a better utilization of seasonally unemployed draught animals, fed on produced fodder. Thus, with very high population density, multi-crop-

[1] See tables in J. Lossing Buck, op. cit., vol. III.

ping provides the advantages of both higher total output and of relatively high output per man-hour compared to annual cropping.

POPULATION GROWTH AND LABOUR PRODUCTIVITY

The purpose of the preceding discussion was to provide an answer to the question whether output per man-hour, as defined, would most likely rise or fall when a given population in a given territory shortens the fallow period and changes its agricultural methods and tools correspondingly. The answer that emerges from this discussion is that output per man-hour is more likely to decline than to increase. This means that in typical cases the cultivator would find it profitable to shift to a more intensive system of land use only when a certain density of population has been reached. In a region where this critical level of density has not yet been reached, people may well be aware of the existence of more intensive methods of land use and they may have access to tools of a less primitive kind; still they may prefer not to use such methods until the point is reached where the size of the population is such that they must accept a decline of output per man-hour.

If it is true, as suggested here, that certain types of technical change will occur only when a certain density of population has been reached, it of course does not follow, conversely, that this technical change will occur whenever the demographic prerequisite is present. It has no doubt happened in many cases that a population, faced with a critically increasing density was without knowledge of any types of fertilization techniques. They might then shorten the period of fallow without any other changes in methods. This constellation would typically lead to a decline of crop yields and sometimes to an exhaustion of land resources. The population would then have to face the choice between starvation and migration.

We know, however, that many different methods of fertilization have been in use all over the world since very ancient times. It must have happened frequently that one people could learn from neighbours or from people they met under migrations in search of unexhausted land, how to preserve crop yields with shorter periods of fallow than those they had used hitherto.[1]

The perspective may be less gloomy for a population which, having reached the critical level of density, ignores the plough—or is unable to use it owing to a lack of suitable animals—although it is aware of the methods of fertilization. This constellation may compel the people in question to accept more steeply diminishing returns to

[1] The big migrations in Europe in the first millennium A.D. seem to have had this effect for many of the migrating tribes.

labour than would have been necessary if they could have changed to plough cultivation, but they may be spared the choice between starvation and migration. Indeed, in this case, the population can continue to increase at the same rate as would have been possible with plough cultivation, especially if irrigation techniques are known.[1]

[1] Some densely peopled regions of pre-Columbian America provide major examples of this.

CHAPTER 5

POPULATION GROWTH AND
WORKING HOURS

It was suggested in the preceding chapters to define the concept of intensification in agriculture in a new way, namely as the gradual change towards patterns of land use which make it possible to crop a given area of land more frequently than before. To re-define intensification in this way is almost tantamount to pointing out that the scope for additional food production in response to population growth is larger than usually assumed.

When a piece of land is to be cropped more frequently—under pre-industrial techniques—it will usually be necessary to devote more agricultural labour to each crop hectare than before. Thus, total agricultural employment is likely to increase for two distinct reasons: the total of cropped area in any given year increases and, at the same time, the annual input of labour per unit of crop area will probably (though not necessarily) increase owing to its being cropped more frequently. It is suggested, furthermore, that, in the typical case, an intensification of the pattern of land use reduces output per man-hour, or, in other words, that agricultural employment increases at a higher rate than agricultural output, when there is a transition to a more intensive kind of land utilization under the pressure of population growth.

The usual definition of intensification is more narrow than the one suggested above. It covers only the use of additional labour per hectare of cropped area, while the change to more frequent cropping of a given area is not regarded as a kind of intensification. In fact, such change in the pattern of land use is not distinguishable—in the traditional view—from the case when virgin land is taken under cultivation. Thus, the failure to grasp the changing role of fallowing distorts the perspective: the additional labour applied to a given crop is viewed not as a means to prevent a decline of crop yields despite the shortening of fallow, but as a means to raise crop yields in order to produce additional food for the growing population. In other words, the important addition to food production and employment obtained by more frequent cropping is liable to be overlooked while attention is focused on the secondary effect, namely the addition to employment resulting from the use of more labour for a given crop. It is obvious that the scope for obtaining additional employment and output by the application of more labour to a given crop is rather narrow. Therefore, this whole reasoning almost unavoidably leads on to a pessimistic view of the possibilities of raising food production and employment in regions, where there is no 'new' land to take into cultivation.

In contrast with this traditional view, the present study endeavours to show that the scope for further intensification (when the term is defined as suggested above) may be very large in regions with little or no virgin land *stricto sensu*. The practical implications of this issue are important, for economists who are unfamiliar with local agricultural conditions tend to underestimate the scope for additional employment and production in agriculture in such regions because they base their reasoning upon an artificial distinction between expansion of cultivation to 'new' land and a much too narrowly defined concept of agricultural intensification. If, in such regions, population is growing at a rapid rate, the further conclusion is usually drawn that sufficient food cannot be produced unless agriculture is equipped with modern means of production from industry, and that the additional rural population cannot be employed in agriculture, but must be transferred to urban activities or remain unemployed or underemployed.

SHORT HOURS UNDER THE LONG-FALLOW SYSTEM

Several different theories have been suggested by economists to explain the low degree of employment that can be observed in the rural areas of many non-industrialized countries. One explanation lays emphasis on the rate of growth of population and suggests that rural underemployment must emerge when the rate of growth of the population becomes so high that the investment necessary for employing additional people cannot be financed. I shall revert to this theory in later chapters.

Another explanation of rural underemployment stresses the degree of population density rather than the rate at which population is growing. According to this explanation, rural underemployment would emerge when settlement has become so dense that the reserve of virgin cultivable land has been used up and quite regardless of whether population is growing rapidly or slowly.[1] On this theory of

---

[1] See note 2, page 31.

underemployment—if it were plausible—we should expect to see a high degree of rural employment in sparsely populated regions and a low degree of employment in very densely populated regions. However, theoretical considerations as well as empirical observations from pre-industrial rural communities lend support to the opposite conclusion.

When the growth of population in a given area of pre-industrial subsistence farming results in lower average output per man-hour in agriculture, the reaction normally to be expected would be an increase of the average number of hours worked per year so as to offset the decline in returns per man-hour. Economists dealing with these matters usually fail to allow for this possibility of responding to diminishing returns by additional work hours rather than by a reduction of food consumption.[1] The reason for this failure to see the possibilities of lengthening the working day in primitive communities is probably to be sought in some vague assumptions to the effect that members of small tribes of very primitive agriculturalists must be working very hard in order to produce and collect food enough for subsistence, or that they are so weakened by insufficient nutrition or malaria that they are unable to work more than they actually do.

However, most studies by anthropologists and others who have been living for long periods among very primitive peoples paint a picture of their daily life which makes it difficult to believe that they fully utilize their capacity for work. The impression left by such studies is that members of sparse tribes of primitive agriculturists usually work much shorter and less regular hours than members of densely settled peasant communities.

Those investigations of which I am aware agree in reporting a very small average labour input per man and year in agriculture under the system of forest fallow. Take for instance Audrey Richards' study of

[1] Professor Arthur Lewis mentions the possibility that reduction of income may be met by harder work, but only to brush it aside as a purely temporary effect: 'In the short run a man has definite ideas of the standard of living which he has to try to maintain, this being the conventional standard of his class . . . if earnings decrease his immediate reaction is to work more. In the longer run, however, his standards are adjustable. If life has become harder, he may lower his standard, and revert to shorter hours. . . . For, it is not only the standard of living that is conventional, but also the number of hours worked. The immediate effect of a change is to leave the standard more or less unchanged, while altering the hours substantially; whereas the ultimate effect is to alter the standard substantially while hours revert towards the previous convention.' W. Arthur Lewis, *The Theory of Economic Growth* (London, 1955), p. 30. It is difficult to understand why Professor Lewis made the assumption that work hours are more conventional in the long run than standards of living. It is at least unlikely to be a realistic assumption in cases where life has become so much harder that people have difficulties in covering their requirements of basic food.

45

the Bemba of Rhodesia, which shows that hours of agricultural work are limited to three to five hours a day. Hoeing is done for only two to four hours. The author stresses the point that there is no such thing as a 'normal working day' among the Bemba, and that daily work, which from being a habit has become almost a physiological necessity for many Europeans, occurs in this type of community only at certain times of the year. Even in the busy season the average working day was found to be only four hours for men and six hours for women. For a less busy season the average for men was 2¾ hours and for women six hours of which only two were devoted to agricultural work while four were spent on domestic activities.[1] Since a great number of days are spent without any agricultural work it is safe to conclude that in the Bemba community the annual average of the performance of work in agriculture (including the clearing of land) amounts to something between one and two hours a day.

Pierre de Schlippe's study of the Zande system of agriculture in Southern Sudan shows a similar picture. The system of cultivation of the Azande was more intensive than that of the Bemba, but also in this tribe the records of work show a very high incidence of leisure. Even in the most busy season, the recordings of the activity 'no work' did not fall below one-fourth to one-fifth of the daily activities recorded and the small input of work in the period contributed to create a hunger period later in the year.[2]

Information from other sources confirm the conclusions reached in the studies quoted above. Forde and Scott's study of South Nigerian agriculture mentions yams cultivators who derive their basic food from one-fifth of a hectare per family and gives information about labour requirements per hectare, which implies that the yams cultivators must be working even shorter hours than the Bemba.[3] The authors of the study conclude that 'where cultivable land is abundant, a considerable surplus of the subsistence crops can be produced without great effort by the ordinary household with

[1] Audrey I. Richards, *Land, Labour and Diet in Northern Rhodesia* (London 1939), pp. 393–5, and table E in the appendix.

[2] 'On July 14th there is a new moon. This one is called *Bamburu*, literally the place which is shorn, or the clearing. It is the last month during which a great effort is made to increase the areas under cultivation. There is a definite improvement in the diet, and therefore strength has come back to the body, whereas the memory of the pangs of hunger is fresh and the effort to avoid its recurrence in the following year is genuine. . . . Now agricultural work reaches its yearly maximum of 54 per cent of the total possible effort, and leisure is reduced to its yearly minimum of 24 per cent.' P. de Schlippe, op. cit., pp. 167–8 and Figs. 17–20 in the appendix, with entrances for work activities and leisure for individual villagers.

[3] Daryll Forde and Scott, op. cit., pp. 81–2 and 91.

customary native methods of cultivation.'[1] The observation that primitive tribes are working short hours is not limited to Africa. Professor Izikowitz' study of the Lamet people in former French Indochina provides us with an example from Asia. The author reports that the Lamet have no hunger periods although 'they seldom work under pressure. The Lamet take life easily and work is discontinued now and then with a pause for sitting and chatting or taking a puff at a smoking pipe.'[2]

Where cultivation under the long-fallow system is a subsidiary occupation, it becomes apparent how little labour is needed to produce the food for a family by this method. In Latin America and parts of Africa, guardsmen of cattle and workers in plantations and European farms are given access to the land belonging to their employers for the purpose of producing food for their own consumption under a system of long fallow. Such people produce the food for themselves and their families with very little work. They can thus devote nearly all of their time to work for their employers, who remunerate them by the provision of non-agricultural goods.

Even where the cultivation system is that of bush fallow combined with permanent cultivation of wet paddy, labour input may remain small by the standard of modern agriculture in western countries. In her economic study of a savannah village in Gambia Miss Haswell found that the men were spending on the average about 700 hours a year on agricultural work, and the women about one-fifth more. Part of this was spent on cash crops exchanged against non-agricultural goods. In the agricultural season the men did on the average six hours of work per working day and the women a little more. But these averages were calculated without inclusion of those days when no agricultural work was done, and these work-less days amounted to nearly two-thirds of the total number of days for men and not much less for women. Moreover, the work was not very regular. A considerable part of the work hours recorded were spent resting in the fields in between the periods of actual work; such periods of rest varied from 10 per cent of total time spent in the fields for a light task such as harvesting to 42 per

[1] Ibid., p. 42. Under the discussion in the Geographical Society in London of a report of a study tour, Professor Daryll Forde made the following remark: 'The people are not underfed in the sense that the volume of food is inadequate, but they are suffering, as people in this country are, from malnutrition. . . . More beans and legumes could be grown and fitted into the existing farm cycle, but the Yakō are not enthusiastic about beans because they mature so late and involve extra weeding, which the women would have to do within the annual cycle.' C. Daryll Forde, 'Land and Labour in a Cross River Village, Southern Nigeria', in *Geographical Journal*, vol. 90 (1937), p. 49.

[2] K. G. Izikowitz, 'Lamet, Hill Peasants in French Indochina', in *Etnologiska Studier* (Göteborg, 1951), No. 17, pp. 262–3.

cent for a heavy task like hoeing. On average, the periods of rest seem to have accounted for around one-fourth of the time spent in the fields.[1]

In some cases of intensive bush fallow the peak may be so busy a period that the family, even when working hard all day, finds it difficult to manage the area needed for subsistence. This is especially so in places where the land has become infested by grasses which make hoeing difficult or require frequent weeding in the rainy season. Examples of this type of very arduous peak-time activity are found in parts of Sudan and Ethiopia, where all family members may be busy weeding from sunrise to sunset during the rainy season.[2]

THE DEAD SEASONS UNDER THE SHORT-FALLOW SYSTEM

When grassy fallow lands, hitherto cultivated with the hoe, are ploughed and used in rotations under short fallow, the seasonal peaks become much more pronounced than they used to be under long fallow. Under the system of bush fallow weeding and collection of fertilizing materials may provide some work outside the most busy seasons of hoeing and harvesting. In addition there is work with the clearing of bush which also falls outside the periods of peak activity. By contrast, under short fallow there is virtually no agricultural work outside the plough season and the harvesting season. Usually the crops are cereals which are neither weeded nor manured apart from the ploughing down of the droppings of the animals, and the animals take care of their own feed by grazing off fallow and permanent grass lands. The plough work replaces both the clearing and the hoeing work, and usually it must be done within a short period, partly because of the condition of the soil and partly in order that the fallow may as long as possible remain available for use by the animals.[3] This latter consideration is important because in large parts of the world the dry period preceding the sowing is the one where it is most difficult for the animals to find sufficient feed.

In dry climates the area which can be cultivated by a family and their beasts is limited by the shortness of the period suitable for ploughing and sowing. For the same reason the area sown varies widely from year to year in dry regions of short-fallow cultivation or

[1] M. R. Haswell, *Economics of Agriculture in a Savannah Village*, Colonial Office (London, 1953, multigraphed). See especially Table 3, p. 25; Table 19, p. 60; and Table 8, p. 43.

[2] According to information by K. M. Barbour, quoted in H. H. Bartlett, 'Fire in Relation to Primitive Agriculture', op. cit., pp. 69 ff.

[3] 'In parts of China the need to plough as late as possible is explained by the strong wind in the winter period, which implies a danger of wind erosion.' T. H. Shen, *Agricultural Resources of China* (New York, 1951), p. 146.

annual cultivation of rain-fed crops. Late sowing is likely to reduce crop yields or even cause a crop failure. Thus, the amount and timing of the downpour in any given year is a major determinant of both the size of the area sown and the yields per unit of land. In humid climates the main seasonal problem arises from the shortness of the period suitable for harvesting rather than of the period for sowing. All the harvesting work may have to be done within a few weeks if destruction by humidity is to be avoided. The tendency, mentioned earlier, to concentrate on cereals under the cultivation system of short fallow makes things worse, because all cereals have nearly the same growing season, and if climatic conditions in any year are unfavourable, all the crops are likely to fail.

These peculiarities of cultivation with short fallow can plausibly explain two characteristic features of communities where the system of short fallow dominates. One of these characteristics is the recurring harvest disasters, which may give rise to serious famines unless large government stocks are kept or food is imported to the region. It must be stressed that the occurrence of famines in such communities does not imply, as is sometimes contended, that the region is overpopulated or the land of poor quality. Nor are these famines to be compared with the hunger periods among primitive tribes which can be ascribed to a lack of effort in agriculture earlier in the year. The cultivators who use the short-fallow system, in dry as well as in humid regions, may have enough land of a reasonable quality and may be toiling hard in the peak seasons; they may nevertheless suffer under famine in years of unfavourable weather.[1]

The second characteristic of systems of short fallow is that they cannot provide agricultural employment for more than a short part of the year, most often about one-third, rarely more than half. The seasonal pattern of work is so pronounced that families who have much more land than they can cope with in the peak season have little to do in most of the remaining part of the year. There is always much underemployment in communities which subsist by the cultivation system of short fallow, but this underemployment is seasonal and it is found also in communities where there is no population pressure on the land.

Most often, those who make quantitative estimates of rural underemployment fail to distinguish between seasonal and other

---

[1] When animals feed mainly on grass, the peasants cannot add much to their total supply of food, reckoned in terms of calories, by killing and eating the animals. It is quite different when the animals are fed on edible roots or cereals since the elimination of the animals will then make vegetable food available for human consumption. Where the animals are kept for draught purposes mainly, the result of reducing their numbers may be famine in subsequent years, when production suffers for lack of draught power.

types of underemployment. Many observers loosely explain agrarian underemployment as a result of overpopulation and make estimates of the amount of underemployment which are nothing but estimates of the average number of days, weeks or months in which the peasants are unoccupied, including both voluntary and seasonal unemployment.

Mr Colin Clark, for instance, has made estimates of agrarian overpopulation in this way. In a paper entitled 'What Constitutes Rural Overpopulation?' he says: 'Take the number of man-hours required per unit area of crop under peasant farming conditions, and then work out the total number of men who can be fully occupied per sq. km. of cultivated land, assuming a 3,000-hour year. For oriental rice growing the figure works out at 42 men per sq. km. of cultivated land, for growing maize (which is a more labour-intensive crop than wheat) in southern and eastern Europe the figure works out at 25.'[1]

Let us try to apply this method to the information about labour requirements for the cultivation of wheat which is available in some very thorough Indian farm surveys. According to these, it would take thirty-three man-days of eight hours to cultivate one hectare of unirrigated wheat in the Punjab, thirty-nine in the State of Bombay and forty-seven in Madhya Pradesh.[2] With Mr Colin Clark's standard of 3,000 hours per year, a cultivator would be able, with his own labour alone, to till annually 11 hectares of dry wheat in the Punjab, 9½ hectares in Bombay and 8 hectares in Madhya Pradesh. But in all these districts land preparation, sowing and harvesting together account for more than 70 per cent of all the labour used; the rest is mainly for threshing and 'watching the crop for birds'. Thus, the operations which have to be done at the beginning and at the end of the growing season together require about one man-month per hectare. Therefore, a man cannot till nearly as large an area as might seem possible on the basis of the method of estimation recommended by Colin Clark. The man must remain unemployed for most of the year unless he can spread the work load by growing some crops with different growing seasons on irrigated land.

Monsoon-fed mono-cultivation of wet paddy is as highly seasonal as the cultivation of dry crops of cereals in semi-arid regions. In the Indian State of West Bengal, the dominant type of paddy

[1] Colin Clark, 'What Constitutes Rural Overpopulation?', in *Proceedings of the Conference on World Population* (Rome, 1954), vol. V (multigraphed edition), p. 229. Later, when Mr Colin Clark was serving as economic adviser to the Government of Pakistan, he applied a standard of full employment of 2,500 hours a year, but apart from this modification, he continued to use the method suggested by him at the Rome conference. See *Report of the Economic Appraisal Committee of the Government of Pakistan* (Karachi, 1953), p. 77.

[2] See the table on page 40.

requires 125 eight-hour man-days per hectare with 40 per cent for preparatory tillage and sowing and 35 per cent for harvest work.[1] In monsoon-fed paddy cultivation without perennial irrigation the preparation of the land and the sowing must be done very quickly when the first showers have made the land suitable. The harvest must also be done very quickly, even if we do not accept the standard of ten to fourteen days proposed by some experts.[2] (Obviously, such standards depend upon the amount of harvest losses which is regarded as tolerable.) Clearly, a Bengal peasant, with this type of production, cannot cultivate nearly as much with his own labour as Mr Colin Clark's calculation would suggest. The very low average level of employment found in many monsoon-fed oriental paddy districts is likely to be due to a very large extent to seasonal unemployment.

THE HARD TOIL OF INTENSIVE AGRICULTURE

The seasonal underemployment which is such a characteristic feature of rural communities based upon the system of short fallow, can be much reduced, if population growth makes it necessary to change over to more intensive types of land use, be it the 'European type' with produced fodder for animals, or the 'Asian type' with irrigation. The reduction of seasonal underemployment in western European agriculture brought about by the change to fodder production and hand feeding of animals in the eighteenth and nineteenth centuries is too well known to need further comment. It should be mentioned, however, that nearly a thousand years before the agricultural revolution seasonal underemployment in much of western European agriculture had been somewhat reduced by the introduction of the three-course rotation of short fallow, which allowed the cultivation of both autumn- and spring-sown crops and thus some spread of operations of ploughing, sowing and harvesting.[3] The famous eighteenth-century revolution in the pattern of employment in European agriculture was therefore a less radical change than the one which may take place when irrigation becomes possible in a hitherto dry region. The improvement of the employment situation made possible by irrigation is particularly striking when the irrigation

---

[1] *Studies in Economics of Farm Management in West Bengal* (Ministry of Food and Agriculture, New Delhi, foreword dated 1959), pp. 244 and 246.

[2] P. Gourou, *L'Utilisation du sol en Indochine française* (Paris, 1940), p. 432; J. Lossing Buck, op. cit., vol. I, p. 13.

[3] The introduction of the three-course rotation in northern Europe in the centuries after A.D. 800 raised total output of agriculture by shortening the periods of fallow and allowed a better seasonal distribution of both human and animal labour, because ploughing for both a spring and an autumn sowing and

is of the perennial type which provides sufficient water in all months of the year.

It was mentioned above that the change from rain-fed to irrigated agriculture involves a large increase in the input of labour. However, part of this additional labour falls in the peak season, and therefore the change can become effective only if the supply of labour can be raised by natural population growth or by the immigration of agricultural labour. But by far the largest share of the additional labour is required in the growing season (watering, weeding and transplanting) or in the dead season between the crops (repair of irrigation facilities and bunds). Indian farm surveys show that when irrigation is introduced the amount of labour required for the period where the crop is growing—which is negligible under the Indian type of dry farming— may increase so as to make up 50 per cent of all the labour required for the crop.[1] Besides the change in the pattern of employment for a given crop, there may be a change to crops with different growing seasons. If multi-cropping is introduced together with the shift from dry to irrigated agriculture the long idle seasons may disappear altogether. The Indian farm surveys illustrate the difference in pattern of employment between regions with little and much irrigation. In a district in West Bengal with 4 per cent of the area irrigated employment in the month of the year where it is lowest is only one-fifth of employment in the months with peak employment, while the corresponding figure is two-fifths in another West Bengal district where 28 per cent of the area is irrigated.[2] A similar picture emerges from the farm surveys of other parts of India.

The unusually high population density in parts of China has made irrigation and multi-cropping much more widespread than it is even in the densely populated districts of India. Accordingly, the employment pattern in most of Chinese agriculture is strikingly different from that of India, despite the fact that there is a pronouncedly cold

---

better spacing of the harvest work became possible. Charles Parain suggests that this change was a means to raise total output because population was increasing: 'As it led to a considerable increase in the total yield of agriculture, the growth of population may often have been a determining factor.' C. Parain, 'The Evolution of Agricultural Techniques', in Cambridge Economic History, op. cit., vol. I, p. 128. Other authors regard the introduction of the three-course rotation as the result of an autonomous invention, which increased labour productivity and can therefore help to explain the subsequent agricultural progress in northern Europe and its contrast with southern Europe. *See* Lynn White jr., 'Technology and Invention in the Middle Ages', in A. F. Havighurst (ed.), *The Pirenne Thesis* (Boston, 1958), p. 81.

[1] See the table on page 40.
[2] 'Studies in Economics of Farm Management in West Bengal', op. cit., pp. 16 and 31.

season in China. According to Lossing Buck's sample study of Chinese agriculture in the 1930s one-third of potential work hours in the four winter months were idle and this idleness accounted for 80 per cent of all rural unemployment in China. The rest of the year had only 5 per cent of rural unemployment and the idle time, including the winter unemployment, was only $1 \cdot 7$ month on the average.[1] Lossing Buck's estimates for China are made in labour-days, supposed to be of about ten hours. Compare this to the very short hours of work in sparsely populated communities of long fallow and to the eight hours which Indian writers usually take as the norm for a full labour-day in India.

THE GRADUAL CHANGE OF WORKING HABITS

Let us boldly surmise, that the amount and pattern of agricultural employment which we find today in sparsely populated regions of underdeveloped countries with systems of extensive land use, give a more or less faithful picture of the pattern and degree of agricultural employment which existed in past times in the now densely populated regions.[2] If this can be accepted as a reasonable historical hypothesis, we may view the changes in agricultural employment brought about by population growth and intensification of land use in a given region as a gradual lengthening of working hours in agriculture.

A thinly spread population begins to do a little agricultural work as a supplement to food collection and hunting. When their territory becomes more crowded they must work more and provide nearly all their food by agricultural work, but this can still be done by a few hours work now and then and requires no regular, daily work. When the further growth of population compels them to change over from forest fallow to bush fallow and to shorten the bush fallow or prolong the periods of cultivation a point is eventually reached where they must accept to do really hard work in one or two relatively short peak seasons. Still, they continue to have long periods with no, or very little, agricultural work. In the long periods of agricultural development before the point is reached where peak activity becomes exceedingly heavy for an ordinary subsistence farmer the individual cultivator could, by working harder, produce more without needing to invest or to change his system of cultivation. However, he is unlikely

[1] J. Lossing Buck, op. cit., vol. I, p. 16, and table in vol. III. See also note 1 on page 104.

[2] English data on farm work in the Middle Ages show that at least in England the working days which the peasants had to perform for the landlords lasted from sunrise to noon only. A fair day's work seems to have been a half-day's work. See B. H. Slicher van Bath, *The Agrarian History of Western Europe* (London, 1963), pp. 183 and 184n.

to do it because he has not yet reached the stage mentioned by Audrey Richards, where daily work from being a habit has become almost a physiological necessity. We may safely assume that he would go in for such changes only under the compulsion of increasing population or under the compulsion of a social hierarchy. This latter possibility—a very real one—will be considered at some length in a later chapter.

The reasoning above will perhaps be met by the objection that the annually recurring hunger periods in some communities living under the system of long fallow are incompatible with the idea that more food could be produced by the average cultivator if only he would agree to reduce his hours of leisure. However, this paradox can be explained in the light of anthropological studies of attitudes in primitive rural communities. Anthropologists stress the lack of foresight and the general inclination to shun hard agricultural work.[1] Economists are perhaps too rash to assume that the primitive cultivators take to food collection only when they are unable to produce food enough for subsistence. Anthropological studies suggest that primitive peoples usually consider both hunting, fishing and food collection as pleasurable activities, while food production is resorted to only to the extent that other and more agreeable activities fail to provide sufficient food. The effort devoted to food production is often seen to be limited to the bare minimum of hours necessary to avoid starvation. This attitude may help to explain why, in communities with a system of long fallow and with abundant land and little input of agricultural labour, the cultivated area is often barely sufficient to give a crop which can last until the following harvest.

The plough, when used for cultivation under short fallow, is a means to preserve the long periods of freedom from agricultural toil even with relatively high densities of population. Cultivators who continue with intensification of long-fallow cultivation beyond a certain stage of population density must work for a longer period of

[1] Audrey Richards summarizes her explanation of the annual hunger periods among the Bemba (North Rhodesia) as follows: 'In conclusion, the Bemba consider it more or less normal for food to be scarce, and both their agricultural system and methods of distribution make it impossible entirely to prevent such a happening. Traditional magic belief teaches that only by supernatural means can the dangers of a shortage be avoided. This firm conviction combined with the temperamental optimism of the Bemba and their lack of interest in hard agricultural work makes them believe that somehow something will happen. . . . The people's system of measurement and their material equipment makes it difficult for them to estimate their supplies exactly, and in any case it does not pay for them to have much more food than their relatives stored in their granaries. All these reasons account for their failure to achieve that attitude of mind which the Europeans describe as "foresight" or "thrift".' Audrey I. Richards, op. cit., p. 208.

the year to obtain the amount of human food that could have been obtained by using a plough. Only when very high population densities have been reached will cultivators using the plough have to give up their periods of seasonal freedom from agricultural work and acquire the habit of regular daily work during long hours all the year round. This stage is not reached before the peasants have to feed their animals nearly all the year on produced fodder or must apply labour intensive irrigation and reap successive crops in order to subsist.

CHAPTER 6

THE COEXISTENCE OF CULTIVATION
SYSTEMS

One of the main contentions of this book is that the growth of population is a major determinant of technological change in agriculture. If this is so, it follows that there must have been some similarity between the rates at which population was growing and the rates at which technological change was occurring. This chapter examines these problems in some more detail, and in the light of historical experience.

Until recently rates of population growth were low or very low in most pre-industrial communities and from time to time the size of the population would be reduced by wars, famines or epidemics. Thus, we should expect the rate of technological change in agriculture to have been slow and interrupted by periods of stagnation or even regression of techniques; before intensive systems of land use had time to become applied over the whole territory of a given village or region, a set-back to population growth might often have occurred and the process of change would be interrupted. Thus, the slowly penetrating new systems of land use and techniques would be expected to coexist for long periods with older systems within the same village or in different villages within the same region.

Is such a theory supported by the available information about past agricultural development and about the present agricultural landscape in underdeveloped countries? In my opinion the hypothesis set forth in this book fits the facts better than does the traditional theory of autonomous technical progress.

Consider, for instance, the spread of the use of the plough.[1] This was an exceedingly slow process. In Europe, the plough was in use several thousand years ago and even in the most remote corners of Europe some ploughs seem to have been in use at least 3,000 years

[1] G. Haudricourt and M. J. Delamarre, *L'homme et la charrue* (Paris, 1955), gives a systematic review of the use of the plough all over the world since antiquity.

56

ago. Stone carvings of ploughs dating from that period have been found as far north as Sweden. Nevertheless, most of Europe seems to have been cultivated by the system of fire, axe and forest fallow as late as the time of the Roman Empire and as late as the eighteenth century it was not uncommon in many villages even in France and Germany that plots in forest and bush land were cleared and cultivated for only a year.[1] Even in the twentieth century, cultivation by forest fallow is found in some mountain districts of central Europe,[2] and until recently, forest fallow was widely used also on flat land in the sparsely populated Scandinavian countries. It was not before the end of the First World War that the burning of forest plots for short-term cultivation ceased in Sweden.[3] Thus, in a country with a rather homogeneous culture like Sweden, where geographical variations in techniques can hardly be explained by a lack of contacts, the plough coexisted with axe and fire for at least 3,000 years.

In Asia, where the plough was used long before it penetrated to Europe, it has never completely replaced fire and axe. There is still some forest fallow in southern China, considerably more in India and very large areas in South East Asia, apart from Java, are under that system of cultivation. The plough has been in use in all these regions for several thousand years, and much cultivation under forest fallow is done by villagers who at the same time use more intensive cultivation systems on part of their village land.

ADAPTATION OF LAND USE TO NATURAL CONDITIONS

In order to understand the process of intensification of land use, it is necessary to take account of the differences in natural conditions for agriculture as between various localities and between different parts of a given village territory. When increasing population density makes it necessary to change the pattern of land use in a given territory the changes are likely to be made in a way which takes account of the differences in natural conditions.

This point may need some explanation. Suppose, for instance, that the population of a community living by the system of forest fallow is increasing and let it be assumed for the sake of simplicity, that the rate at which the population is growing is relatively low, but regular.

[1] Marc Bloch, op. cit., vol. I (Paris, 1931), pp. 26–30, and vol. II (Paris, 1956), pp. 23–6, 33–8 and 68–75.

[2] Statistics of the area under the cultivation system of forest fallow in central Europe around 1900 are available in the article 'Haubergwirtschaft', in *Handwörterbuch der Staatswissenschaften*, vol. IV (Jena, 1900), pp. 1123–4.

[3] H. C. Darby, 'The Clearing of the Woodland in Europe', in W. L. Thomas, op. cit., p. 210.

Our cultivators would begin by gradually spreading their cultivation —under the system of forest fallow—over the territory under their command. At a certain point, when they have become so numerous that it is getting difficult to find suitable forest, they would begin to shorten the period of fallow and cultivate first a little part of the land, but later more and more of it, with the system of bush fallow instead of that of forest fallow. If they are aware of plough techniques and have access to draught animals they are unlikely to proceed far with the intensification of bush fallow. Instead, they may prefer to clear a few plots more thoroughly, removing stones and roots, and begin to use them in a system of short fallow with ploughing while they continue with long fallow in most of the area. Further fields for ploughing would be prepared in step with the increase of population. If the rate of population growth were very low, the complete change from one cultivation system to another might take many centuries.

At the time when our community was still relatively sparsely populated and the plough was being slowly introduced in replacement of long fallow, a few arable fields would be prepared each year, or at longer intervals, and the number of temporary plots cleared annually in the forest would be reduced a little, so as to prevent the complete disappearance of the forest. Centuries later, when our community had become much more densely populated, and for instance was replacing short-fallow cultivation with annual cropping of irrigated land, a few fields would each year—or at longer intervals —be provided with irrigation facilities and some dry fields would be allowed to lapse into a state of permanent grazing, so as to provide fodder for the necessary increase in the number of domestic animals. Finally, when our community had become extremely densely populated a few fields would now and then be added to the part of that cultivated area, which could be sown and harvested twice a year instead of once, or three times instead of two. If the rate of population growth was sufficiently low, an observer at any given moment would not see many signs of change. He would be inclined to describe the community as technically stagnant.

At every stage of this process of transformation, the fields first chosen for more frequent cropping would be among those relatively well suited for the next step in the development towards more intensive patterns of land use. This would be flat fields at the stage when plough cultivation was to be introduced, it would be land near rivers or wells when annual cropping with irrigation was to appear, and at the point of transition to intensive manuring, fields close to centres of settlement would be chosen for the conversion.

Once a particular system of land use had become the dominant one, the fields still under the previous system would probably not be particularly well suited for the new system of land use. Some cultivators might therefore find it preferable to introduce a third, and still more intensive system, instead of continuing with the shift away from the oldest and most extensive system to the one of intermediate intensity. There would then be three systems of land use coexisting in the same village territory, each of them occupying land which seemed relatively well suited for that particular degree of intensity.[1]

A contemporary observer, who were to make a cross-section survey of the village territory at any given moment during this period of gradual change, would perhaps be inclined to interprete it in terms of a static geographic theory of land use. He would explain that different types of land use were adaptations to differences in natural conditions, because each part of the village territory seemed to be used in the way for which it was best suited. If our observer happened to be a staunch Malthusian he would point out with conviction that the differences in intensity of land use had developed because the population had grown up to the size which could be supported in a territory with these particular natural conditions; and he might go on to say that it would be impossible to apply more labour productively in that territory, and that additional population would have to face the choice between underemployment and starvation, or emigration.

THE CASES OF JAVA AND JAPAN

Dutch observers have many times taken such cross-section views of the island of Java and concluded from the dense population in the fertile volcanic districts that the island was overpopulated.[2] Such a statement was made already one and a half centuries ago[3] but today the number of inhabitants is more than ten times as large; and Java is nearly self-sufficient in food, even though hardly any chemical fertilizer is used for food production.

The striking expansion of agricultural production in Java is some-

[1] A. T. Grove has made the observation that where population densities in Northern Nigeria are below the range of 150–200 to the square mile, the pattern of land utilization is largely unrelated to variations in the inherent capabilities of land resources, but any particular patch may be under woodland at one time, rough grazing at another, cropped for a few years and then abandoned while in areas with higher population densities land use is much more closely correlated with variations of soil conditions. See A. T. Grove, 'Population Densities and Agriculture in Northern Nigeria', in Barbour and Prothero, op. cit., pp. 125–6.

[2] For a recent example of this see F. A. van Baaren, 'Soils in Relation to Population in Tropical Regions', in *Tijdschrift voor Economische en Sociale Geografie* (Rotterdam, September 1960).

[3] In 1816, a former director of the province of Java's North-East Coast remarked that in his time the rice fields were cultivated on rotation because the 'population far exceeded the cultivation'. (Quoted from J. M. van der Kroef, *Indonesia in the Modern World*, vol. II (Bandung, 1956), p. 67.)

times explained as the result of the agricultural education and the capital investment undertaken by the Dutch. But these activities can account for only a small share of the additional food production in the island. The main explanation of the high elasticity of production is in the gradual spread over the island of methods applied in parts of its territory for centuries before the arrival of the Dutch.

The cultural pattern of Java is rather homogeneous, and it is impossible to explain geographical differences in technical methods within the island in terms of insufficient cultural contacts. The plough was in use in the tenth century and it was probably introduced much earlier. When the Dutch arrived, most of the island was still under the systems of forest and bush fallow, but long fallow has gradually been eliminated as a result of the rapid growth of population in the Dutch period. Systematic comparison of reports from various periods of the colonial era has revealed successive changes in some areas from long fallow to short fallow and from short fallow to annual and multiple cropping.

The changes that took place in Java are well summarized by H. Bartlett: 'During the last century typical *ladang* cultivation (i.e. long-fallow cultivation) as it persists elsewhere in Indonesia fell more and more into disuse on account of the great pressure on land that arose from excessive increase in the population and finally practically disappeared. *Ladang* land of the sort that required felling and burning of forest and a long recovery period of ten or twenty years after from one to three seasons of satisfactory agricultural productivity, ceased to exist, being replaced by the permanent cultivation of dry fields . . . when *ladang* cultivation evolved through necessity into a higher type of land use. Before *ladang* cultivation with a forest fallow was abandoned it sometimes went into a limited phase of long grass-land fallow, which could only exist where excessive expenditure of labour was made necessary by dearth of suitable land.'[1] Commenting on the Government report of 1911 for Middle Java he says: 'This entire report is interesting as indicating what happens, when population pressure finally becomes too great after a long period of unplanned land use, or abuse. Forest is swept into grass land. By excessive grazing useless bushy and thorny wooded vegetation is enabled to take over the grass land. Permanent agriculture on non-irrigated land supersedes the primitive shifting agriculture through various intervening stages in which the labour demand grows, the fallow stages grow short and finally, by unwilling adoption of deep cultivation and manuring, the stage of annual cropping is reached, but by a wasteful and devastating series of steps.'[2]

[1] H. H. Bartlett, 'Fire in Relation to Primitive Agriculture', op. cit., p. 554.
[2] Ibid., p. 807. See also pp. 158, 651, 721 and 801–9.

Today long fallow has nearly vanished from Java and multiple cropping has become widespread in the most densely populated parts of the island. In step with these changes, the Javanese peasant has been transformed from the careless idler of the old times, who had just to scratch the land to get food enough. In the most densely populated regions the peasants of today are working hard in tiny fields in order to keep them completely free of weeds and so level that no water runs to waste or damages the crop.

The agriculture of Japan in the period from about 1600 to about 1850 provides another example of rising population and gradual change to more intensive systems of land use.[1] At the beginning of the period dynastic change created internal peace after a period of turbulence, and population grew rapidly, particularly during the first half of the period. From a certain point, the increase of population seems to have caused a reduction of the average size of agricultural holdings and a thorough change of methods. Ploughing with the help of draught animals became more frequent, and double cropping was made possible by irrigation and by the use of purchased night soil and dried fish for fertilizer as a supplement to or substitution for the traditional method of trampling grass, leaves or ashes into the fields. A number of publications propagated improved methods of farming and the spreading of new crops and varieties.

Thomas C. Smith makes it clear, in his interesting analysis of Japanese agriculture in this period, that few of these changes were the result of contemporary inventions; most of them resulted from the spread of known techniques from localities where they were already well established to areas where they had been unknown or unused. He also emphasizes that for the majority of the holdings the effect of the changes was to raise not only yields per hectare, but also labour requirements per hectare. Nevertheless, he thinks that the cause of the changes 'remains obscure' and he explicitly rejects the idea that population increase was the driving force. His main argument against such an explanation is that the bulk of the population increase came before 1725, whereas both the technical changes and the trend towards smaller holdings were most marked after that time.[2] This argument, however, is not wholly convincing since there may have been considerable scope around 1600 for the accommodation of additional people and increased production of food without the recourse to subdivision of existing holdings with use of intensive methods. These became indispensable at a later stage, when the density of population had reached a certain critical level.

---

[1] Thomas C. Smith, *The Agrarian Origins of Modern Japan* (Stanford University Press, 1959). See especially the chapter on agricultural technology, pp. 87–107.

[2] Ibid., pp. 87 and 104–5.

REDUCTIONS OF POPULATION DENSITY

In both Java and Japan the size of populations was steadily growing for several centuries. This, however, is somewhat exceptional; agrarian history knows relatively few examples of such steady growth and many more of population growth interrupted by frequent set-backs, as already mentioned. According to Malthusian theory we would expect population quickly to regain its former size after such set-backs, but historical evidence does not confirm this expectation. It took a century to regain the losses after the Thirty Years' War in central Europe and there are many examples from all parts of the world of still longer periods of recuperation.

In cases where population density was reduced by wars or other catastrophes there often seems to have been a relapse into more extensive systems of cultivation. Many of the permanent fields which were abandoned after wars or epidemics during the early Middle Ages remained uncultivated for centuries after. The use of labour-intensive methods of fertilization, such as marling, were abandoned for several centuries in France and then reappeared in the same region, when population again became dense.[1] The disappearance and reappearance of the cultivation of leguminous crops have already been mentioned.

Latin America is the region which suffered most from population decline in recent centuries. In many regions, the population density of pre-Columbian times has never been regained and the Indian population has regressed in agricultural techniques. More revealingly, the same process of technical regression can be seen, when migrants from more densely populated regions with much higher technical levels become settlers in the sparsely populated regions of Latin America. Let me illustrate this by quoting the statement made at an international conference by a specialist on rural conditions in Latin America:

'It seems to me that two points should be made. First of all, as most of us realize, a large proportion of all of the farmed area and of the farm population of Latin America is in a pre-scientific stage. . . .

[1] During the period of population increase in England and some parts of France in the sixteenth century, marl and lime were put on the land for the first time since the Roman period and the thirteenth century (i.e. the two previous periods of high population densities). See B. H. Slicher van Bath, op. cit., p. 205. In regions of northern Germany, where the land before the Thirty Years' War had been fallowed only every fourth, fifth, sixth or eighth year, the population decline caused by the war led to a return to the three-course rotation, which survived in these regions until the eighteenth century. Ibid., p. 245. See also the enumeration of the eleven systems of land use which coexisted in western Europe in the seventeenth and eighteenth centuries. Ibid., p. 244.

This is because the people are isolated by distance, or by completely different cultural levels, or by cultural inertia—defined as the reluctance of a conservative rural society to adopt new ideas. . . . The other point I would like to make is that there are certain segments of the Latin American farm population which according to field investigators have been descending in the technological scale rather than ascending. They are going the wrong way. Observers such as Waibel and Lynn Smith, who have studied the relatively recent European colonization in South Brazil, for example, tell us that these colonists, who came (or whose ancestors came) from countries like Germany and Italy with relatively advanced techniques, have lost many of these techniques. This is true even of such fairly simple practices as the use of the plow and crop rotation and the inclusion of livestock and forage crops in the farm economy for the maintenance of soil fertility.'[1]

This Latin American experience of apparent technical regression, when population declines or when people move to less densely populated areas, is by no means unique.[2] Many observers report of apparent technical regression after migrations to less densely populated regions even in cases where the migrations took place at government initiative and were designed to promote the spread of intensive methods to the regions of immigration. In both Tanganyika, Vietnam, Ceylon and India extension service administrations have made the experience that cultivators who used intensive methods in their densely settled home districts give up these methods after they have been resettled in less densely populated districts and given more land per family. Many settlement areas, meant to serve as model farms for the local population, provide sad sights of poor yields obtained from unweeded and unwatered fields.

EFFECTS OF RAPID POPULATION GROWTH

The examples above referred partly to the case of a steady but relatively slow population increase accompanied by changes of agricultural techniques, and partly to the case of a decline of population or migration to less densely populated regions accompanied by a return

[1] See the statement made by Henry S. Sterling at the 1951 International Conference on Land Tenure and Related Problems in World Agriculture. Kenneth H. Parsons et al. (ed.), *Land Tenure* (Madison, 1956), pp. 349–50.

[2] Professor Sauvy is emphatic on this point: 'On ne peut trouver, dans l'histoire, aucune stagnation ou recul démographique heureux. Une telle accumulation de démentis montre que la théorie est défectueuse, pèche par quelque point.' A. Sauvy, *Théorie générale de la population*, vol. II (Paris, 1954), p. 20. P. Gourou gives examples of a return to extensive land use in 'Les pays tropicaux', op. cit., pp. 101, 109 and 142.

to extensive and apparently more primitive techniques. It now remains to consider the effects of very rapid population growth on agricultural methods.

With rapid population growth, the process of intensification would need to take place much more quickly than in the cases we have dealt with so far. Not just a few fields, but a large number of fields would each year have to be cleared or provided with irrigation facilities, perhaps with the result that two harvests could be taken annually rather than one. A large amount of land clearing, land improvement and drainage or investment in irrigation facilities would have to take place simultaneously. Contemporary observers would not fail to notice this increased activity and they might well describe the period of rapidly rising population as a period of agricultural revolution. The agricultural revolution in eighteenth-century western Europe seems to have been of this type, and the agricultural changes which are now occurring in many underdeveloped countries seem to provide us with another example of rapid spread of the techniques of intensive agriculture owing to population pressure. Future historians will perhaps describe the decades after 1950 as those of the Indian agrarian revolution.

When population growth becomes so rapid, in a pre-industrial economy, that its effects may appear as an agricultural revolution to contemporary observers or economic historians, new and difficult problems, unknown under slow or moderate growth, present themselves. The cultivators must be able to adapt themselves quickly to methods which are new to them, although they may have been used for millenia in other parts of the world, and—perhaps even more difficult—they must get accustomed, within a relatively short period, to regular, hard work instead of a more leisurely life with long periods of seasonal idleness. Moreover, the community must somehow be able to bear the burden of a high rate of investment and perhaps to undertake sweeping changes in land tenure. I shall revert to the problems of investment and land tenure in later chapters.

CHAPTER 7

DIMINISHING RETURNS TO LABOUR
AND TECHNICAL INERTIA

If we accept the idea that a certain density of population is a pre-
condition for the introduction of given techniques, a number of
facts which have puzzled colonial officers and government officials
in underdeveloped countries appear in a new light.

The general belief that ignorance is the chief cause of the use of
extensive methods of cultivation made colonial as well as independent governments anxious to instruct primitive cultivators in the use
of intensive methods of production. It is true that the colonial powers
were interested in promoting the output of commercial crops more
than in the progress of food production, but some of them nevertheless established a network of advisers to teach the cultivators to till
their land more intensively and with less primitive methods. Such
attempts at agricultural education were sometimes successful, in
other cases their failure was conspicuous. In some cases cultivators
under the system of long fallow refused to abandon fire and take to
the plough; in other cases, cultivators living with the system of
short fallow failed to use the water from new irrigation canals provided by the colonial governments and refused to change to more
frequent cropping of irrigated land.

Some of the newly independent governments in former colonies
have organized extension services on a much larger scale than was
attempted in the colonial period, but often the results have been just
as disappointing as in earlier periods. In some villages and with some
groups of producers the extension officers obtain encouraging results,
but there are many complaints about stubborn resistance to changes
of methods suggested by the new advisers.[1]

Most often, the extension programme of a given country consists

---

[1] See the periodic *Evaluation Report on the Working of Community Projects
and National Extension Service Blocks* (Government of India, New Delhi),
passim.

B

of a set of standard recommendations, and not all extension officers can establish the true costs of the recommended changes in the specific area in which they are working. Measures are sometimes recommended just because they have been successful elsewhere, perhaps in communities with a quite different density of population.[1] Extension officers and visiting experts often appear to be thinking mainly in terms of technical potentialities for better land utilization and higher total output and underestimate the cost in additional labour both for current operations and for investment, which the new methods would entail.

One of the misconceptions that tend to mislead advisers is the general belief that there is an excessive supply of labour in rural districts of underdeveloped countries. Technical advisers who are unfamiliar with the conditions of the local labour market often seem to take it for granted that the cultivators have a preference for regular employment and are willing to give up seasonal leisure for a very modest compensation in additional output. They assume that labour intensive practices can easily be introduced by education and instruction, if they can be performed in the idle season.[2]

But the cultivators do not forget or neglect the additional labour they would have to perform if they accepted the advice. Reports of extension officers, both from the colonial period and more recent ones, give numerous examples of cultivators who refuse to introduce ploughing or transplanting or production of fodder or other changes suggested by the advisers with the explicit motivation that this would add too much to the labour with the crop. Such objections are often interpreted as a lack of interest in raising total income, but it may be suggested that they can more plausibly be explained as the result of a quite rational comparison between the additional labour and the probable addition to output.

Thus, it may be sound economic reasoning rather than indolence which induces a community of cultivators under the system of long fallow to refuse to abandon fire and axe, when they are offered help to change to plough culture, and instead to move to another place in the forest, where there is still room for the system of long fallow. Con-

---

[1] The administration of the Indian programme of community development was criticized for taking insufficient account of local conditions in its recommendations. *Report of a Community Development Evaluation Mission in India*, United Nations (New York, 1959), p. 32.

[2] An extreme example of this view is found in the study of rural underemployment undertaken by Wilbert Moore for the League of Nations: 'Increased productivity per man-hour is no advantage for the peasant family whose labour supply is in a sense part of its fixed costs.' Wilbert E. Moore, *Economic Demography of Eastern and Southern Europe* (League of Nations, Geneva, 1945), p. 109.

versely, sound economic reasoning may persuade another community, which is unable to find suitable land for continued cultivation under long fallow, to accept the help and take to ploughing of permanent fields. Peasants with too little land for cultivation with short fallow and with no other employment opportunities behave rationally when they use the water from irrigation canals and change to more intensive cultivation, but peasants with land enough for short-fallow cultivation may be equally justified in finding that the addition to output which can be obtained by watering the crop is an insufficient reward for the reduction of the customary seasonal leisure.

Both in the colonial period and later, the many failures in the attempts to introduce apparently superior methods and tools made officials and social scientists wonder whether there could be something wrong with the basic theory. It seemed obvious that the continued use of primitive methods could not be due to ignorance alone, when the cultivators so often refused to change them, when offered government aid of various types, ranging from advice to direct subsidies and supply of equipment.

Already in the colonial period, anthropologists and other social scientists, familiar with the customs of primitive peoples, suggested that the persistence of the traditional methods was an indication not of ignorance, but of the fact that primitive tribes and villagers were unresponsive to economic incentives and preferred to behave in the traditional way, also when it was against their economic interest.[1] The disappointing results obtained by many extension service organizations after independent governments have been established have lent new colour to this questionable theory.

It is undeniable that many people hesitate to change accustomed methods unless economic incentives are very strong, and it is possible that this attitude is more widespread in primitive communities than in more advanced. But on the other hand an impressive amount of evidence is available to show that there can be a great willingness to respond to economic incentives even in the most primitive communities.[2] New crops were eagerly accepted both when the Portu-

---

[1] An outstanding exponent of this theory was J. H. Boeke, see especially his *Economics and Economic Policy of Dual Societies* (Haarlem, 1953).

[2] This view, which contrasts vividly with that of J. H. Boeke and his Dutch followers, was propounded by J. S. Furnivall: 'Yet the Dutch picture of a native world, in which economic values are disregarded, seems, so far as it is based on facts, to be drawn from Java, where for some two hundred years employers secured labour through compulsion rather than by appealing to the desire of gain. In Africa likewise . . . a popular belief in the native disregard of economic values has been held to justify compulsion as a means of securing labour. But everywhere experience has shown that the desire of gain can easily be stimulated or, rather, liberated from the control of custom. In British colonies under

guese brought new crops to Africa and Asia and much more recently.[1] Crops like maize, cassava and potatoes have spread very rapidly in primitive communities in recent decades also where they were un-aided by government propaganda. Commercial crops have also been accepted readily when production was profitable, although the cultivation of them by native cultivators was often resented by the plantation companies and obstructed in various ways by the colonial governments.

In accordance with this kind of experience, many anthropologists and other experts take exception from the idea of a strong preference for customary behaviour.[2] Some even complain of the strong appeal of profit in primitive communities. Accustomed cultural and social patterns are said to distintegrate much too quickly under the lure of profit, with the result that age-old traditions of tribal solidarity and mutual aid collapse, leaving the weaker members of the communities unprotected.

Thus, empirical evidence is contradictory. In some cases at least, the contradiction may be due to different strength of the economic incentive because of differences in population trends or other factors. I suggest, therefore, that in cases where we observe resistance to technical change, the economist should not leave the explanation to be offered by anthropologists, sociologists or social psychologists before he has investigated whether he is faced with a case where technical change would be associated with diminishing returns to

---

indirect rule, interpreted according to the British tradition of the rule of law, economic forces soon permeate the native world. . . .' J. S. Furnivall, *Colonial Policy and Practice* (Cambridge, 1957), p. 304.

[1] 'Maize, cassava, groundnuts, sweet potatoes, tobacco and chillies are of American origin and have reached the African west coast some time in the sixteenth or seventeenth century. They have penetrated into Central Africa ahead of European occupation. The exact time of their appearance in Zandeland (Southern Sudan. E.B.) is not known.' P. de Schlippe, op. cit., p. 262.

[2] Two of the social anthropologists quoted in previous chapters, S. F. Nadel and Audrey Richards, belong to this group. Nadel says: 'The fact that the Nupe farmer is go-ahead with respect to certain farm techniques and "conservative" with respect to others is not due to any tribal or racial "conservatism", but reveals itself as a clear instance of the working of free economic choice.' S. F. Nadel, op. cit., p. 237. Audrey Richards says: 'The primitive cultivator is often said to follow tribal tradition blindly, without choice or reason, but in actual fact when seen in his own garden he appears as a man struggling in a hard environment with a bewildering number of alternative courses of action, and there are as many grades between the fool and the wise man as in any community of our own. The conservatism of the tribal African has, I think, been exaggerated. In reality, most of the Bantu have been changing their agricultural practices in contact with the surrounding peoples for generations, and a good many experiments are actually made in the course of an individual's life.' Audrey I. Richards, op. cit., pp. 229–30.

labour, so that the resistance to change need not be explained in terms of a failure to respond to genuine economic incentives.[1]

[1] In fact, several of the detailed economic studies mentioned in previous chapters conclude that intensive cultivation is unremunerative in the districts studied and that, therefore, the cultivators behave with economical rationality when they prefer extensive cultivation methods. Miss Haswell concludes her analysis as follows: 'The analysis of labour costs of millet production . . . leads to a conclusion which seems to be of outstanding importance . . . high intensity of production does not lead to low labour costs . . . by and large, there seems to be little reduction in cost as a result of more intensive practices. Thus, it may well be that the Genieri people, and many other African people in similar circumstances, have no apparent incentive to use their food grain lands better.' M. R. Haswell, op. cit., p. 55. Among the six Indian farm management studies carried out in the period 1956–7, two had to conclude that intensive cultivation was uneconomic in the districts covered. The Madras report has this to say: 'On the whole, the position was better in the year under report largely owing to the rise of prices. But it is a little surprising that in the three irrigated crops . . . losses had to be incurred. In irrigated crops generally the output is higher than in the unirrigated crop, but the higher output is usually secured with too high a rate of input with the result that the total cost remains uncovered.' *Studies in Economics of Farm Management in Madras* (Ministry of Food and Agriculture, New Delhi, foreword dated 1960), p. 191. The report for West Bengal, in a chapter on 'Economy of the Farm', concludes as follows: 'The profit analysis has clearly brought out the most disturbing feature of the present system of cultivation, namely, the tendency of the profit to decline with increase in inputs.' *Studies in Economics of Farm Management in West Bengal*, op. cit., p. 80.

CHAPTER 8

THE VICIOUS CIRCLE OF SPARSE POPULATION AND PRIMITIVE TECHNIQUES

Up to this point, the productive activities other than food production were ignored. We must now give up this simplification in order to get a fuller and more realistic view of the development of rural communities under the pressure of increasing population. Systems of land use and cultivation can be fully understood only if they are considered as one part of the pattern of social organization as a whole.

Under the system of forest fallow, the cultivators can produce food for their own consumption with comparatively little toil and trouble. But they need a large area of land per family—including of course the land laying fallow at any given time—and they must therefore be thinly spread over the territory, grouped in relatively small communities. Within such small and widely-scattered groups, only a rudimental division of labour is possible, and therefore activities like the production of tools, weapons, household goods and clothing are time-consuming and rarely develop to a high level of perfection. The long distances to communities of higher civilization make it impossible, or at least uneconomical, to acquire such goods in exchange against basic foods. Therefore, in communities of forest fallow the production of food surpluses, though potentially large, occurs in actual fact only in those cases where such tribes happen to live near to plantations or mines so that they have a market within easy reach.

The need to move cultivation from one plot to another every year and to find plots which have rested for a generation or more, makes it necessary to remove or rebuild the huts at frequent intervals. This precludes a settled community life, and an elaborate social organization is unlikely to develop under such conditions. In other words, the exigencies of the system of forest fallow can go a long way to explain the chief characteristics of the tribal way of life : a primitive existence

70

in small unsettled groups, where there is no intricate social hierarchy and no central authority, although tribal chiefs may exert some authority and on certain occasions receive conventional and ceremonial gifts from the members of the tribe.

With the transition to the system of bush fallow there is a tendency for settlement to become more stable and for the average size of local communities to become larger. Some division of labour is likely to develop, and village markets may appear, where more or less accidental surpluses of food are exchanged against non-agricultural goods. But at this stage the producers of non-agricultural goods are rarely full-time artisans, they use part of their time in food production. As long as the villages continue to be moved from time to time, the division of labour must remain limited and the level of productivity in non-agricultural activities must be low. Permanent village roads do not exist, transport is time-consuming and inefficient. If village markets exist, the supplies brought to them are only small.

With the creation of permanent fields, cleared of roots and stones, permanent habitations are established in their vicinity. Under the system of short fallow cultivators will always be found to have settled in villages or individual habitations which are meant to be permanent. The transition to permanent settlement helps to develop non-agricultural activities. Instead of temporary huts, durable houses are built; it becomes worthwhile to construct roads and to sink wells for drinking water, and a social framework emerges within which professional artisans and traders can develop a more lasting and specialized activity. In short, tribal organization gives way to more differentiated forms of social organization.

With further increase in the density of population and with the shift to intensive systems of land utilization the region is likely to become urbanized to some extent. The pre-conditions for urbanization are not only that agriculture is able to produce a surplus of basic foods, but also that population density is relatively high. It is true, of course, that output per man-hour in agriculture tends to decline with increasing population density, but (as explained in chapter 5) this decline is likely to be offset, more or less, by longer hours. Therefore, a large agricultural population within a given territory under pre-industrial systems of cultivation can support an absolutely larger non-agricultural population than a smaller one.[1] Moreover, for the non-agricultural population to concentrate

[1] Many authors consider the growth of towns in Europe in the eleventh and twelfth centuries to have been caused by preceding technical inventions in agriculture. It was, however, part of an overall increase of population resulting from pacification after centuries of wars, invasions and internal unrest. See Henri Pirenne, *Medieval Cities* (New York, Anchor, A 82), p. 55. The increase of rural population was accompanied by large clearings of forest land and by a

in real towns a certain critical level of population density must have been reached. This is so, because only in a densely populated region can a relatively efficient transport system exist without absorbing an inordinate share of the total labour force. Regular food transport to large towns is therefore possible only when relatively high population densities have been reached. It is therefore unwarranted to take the low degree of urbanization in regions of long-fallow agriculture as an indication of a low output per man-hour in agriculture.[1]

PRE-CONDITIONS FOR THE CONCENTRATION OF POPULATION

It is common knowledge that the division of labour and hence the productivity of non-agricultural activities depend upon the density of settlement. But as long as the true importance of the cultivation system of long fallow was not recognized, it was too easily assumed that a small population could reap the benefits of the division of labour by just drawing together in a small part of its territory. The assumption was that a small group would begin by cultivating a small area either of the most fertile or the most easily cultivable land within the territory it dominated.

In actual fact, however, it is unlikely that a small agricultural population would concentrate voluntarily. In typical cases, a small population can obtain its food by a much smaller input of labour if, instead of crowding together on a part of the territory, they spread widely, with an average population density of one family or two per square kilometre. Such a scattered population may be in contact with neighbouring peoples with other methods of cultivation and much higher cultural levels and may from them receive better axes and hoes than they could make themselves, but it is unlikely that they would emulate their agricultural methods, since this would usually entail an immediate reduction of output per man-hour. They would

---

spread of the three-course rotation of short fallow mentioned in note 1, page 62. It would seem that these agricultural changes would make it possible to feed a much more numerous urban population, even if there would be no increase of annual output per man in agriculture, and thus little change in the *share* of total population not needed for food production.

[1] The following statement provides an example of this approach. 'The productivity of African agriculture is still so low that it takes anywhere from two to ten people—men, women and children—to raise enough food to supply their own needs and those of one additional—non-food-growing—adult. If we take six as the average, this means that of the estimated 120 million people of working age (eight and over), not more than 20 million are able to leave their lands at any one time, without seriously upsetting the traditional economy.' George H. T. Kimble, *Tropical Africa* (abridged edition, vol. I, New York, 1962), p. 481.

be forced to work harder in order to obtain advantages which to them would not appear as necessarily connected with a change in their system of food production. The difficulty is that the advantages of dense and permanent settlement, which are undoubtedly large, are not reaped from one day to another. They appear very slowly, while the disadvantages of concentration appear immediately in the form of harder and longer working hours spent on cultivation and on investment in land improvement.

It thus appears that a population which is small in relation to the total territory it commands, cannot owing to this very smallness get into a process of economic and cultural development. Both ancient and more recent history lend colour to the suggestion that a concentration of population, accompanied by the change to intensive systems of cultivation, will take place only under the pressure of increasing populations or when a tribe or people can force captured slaves to work harder in agriculture than free members of tribal communities are prepared to do.

It is a fair generalization to say that all the ancient communities which applied intensive systems of land utilization used servile labour, usually captives of war and descendents of such captives. These were the men and women who performed the toil of investment as well as much of the current work in agriculture. Where population is sparse and fertile land abundant and uncontrolled, a social hierarchy can be maintained only by direct, personal control over the members of the lower class. In such communities therefore, both subjugated peoples and individual captives of war are kept in personal bondage. Bonded labour is a characteristic feature of communities with a hierarchic structure, but surrounded by so much uncontrolled land suitable for cultivation by long-fallow methods that it is impossible to prevent the members of the lower class from finding alternative means of subsistence unless they are made personally unfree. When population becomes so dense that the land can be controlled, it becomes unnecessary to keep the lower class in personal bondage; it is sufficient to deprive the working classes of the right to be independent cultivators.

We need not go back to the ancient history of Europe, Asia or America in order to see the close relationship between sparse population, long-fallow cultivation and the existence of slavery. When the Europeans arrived in Africa, domestic and agricultural slaves were numerous in many parts of the continent and administrative centres and trading towns were supplied with food from large land holdings with servile labour. Even today, long after the legal abolition of slavery in European colonies, 'clients' and 'attached labourers', who differ from slaves in little but the name, are numerous in parts of

Africa and in some other parts of the world. Many wives in poly-gamic tribes are domestic and agricultural slaves in disguise.

During the days of slavery in Africa, and probably elsewhere too, the slaves were obtained by raids among neighbouring, numerically weaker tribes living by the system of long fallow. A tribe, which for some reason had a more rapid rate of growth than its neighbours, was not faced with the choice between starvation and conquest of territory, as those following a Malthusian line of thought might expect. Instead, the young men of the tribe would set out to capture additional labour outside their own territory and put them to agricultural work. In this way, taking advantage of their larger numbers by enslaving members of neighbouring tribes, a tribe with rapid growth of population could secure for itself the advantages of dense and permanent settlement while avoiding the burden of ad-ditional hard work in agriculture. Thus, a beginning of economic development would be achieved by the method of increasing the population through imports of slave labour. In fact, population in-crease is a condition for economic development in its first stages.[1]

The slave raids of old times had the effect of increasing the con-trast in population densities and levels of civilization as between neighbouring tribes and peoples. The numerically weak were fre-quently decimated by the slave raiders and those left behind could easily find subsistence by means of long-fallow systems with the result that they were never able to break the vicious circle of sparse population, long-fallow agriculture and low levels of civilization.[2] They continued, sometimes for millennia, to serve as reservoirs of potential slave labour for their more prolific neighbours. The numerically strong became still stronger, because they could use the

[1] If slaves are unavailable, numbers may be increased by adoption of children. 'There is a bump of philoprogenitiveness in the population which has been relatively wealthy, and households have been artificially increased by buying . . . children to enlarge the family and the kin-group.' C. Daryll Forde, 'Land and Labour in a Cross River Village', op. cit., p. 50.

[2] The slave raids for the benefit of the American market caused a set-back to population density in the regions of Africa which were most severely hit. It is probable that for that reason forest and bush could become denser in the regions around the trade routes, and this may have been one of the factors which retarded the change-over from long-fallow systems to plough cultivation with animal draught power in Central Africa. It would seem more natural to look for the cause of the slow penetration of the plough in Africa in the low population density than to brush it aside with the usual reference to 'ignorance of the plough in Africa'. The latter explanation seems difficult to reconcile with the fact that there were many contacts between Abyssinia, North Africa and Guinea, where the plough was used, and regions where it was (and is) unused. See also note 1, page 68, where the spread of American crops from West Africa to Central and East Africa is mentioned.

slaves to produce their food and other necessities and thus concentrate on the art of war.[1] Sometimes the toil of the slaves made it possible for a leisured class with a high urban civilization to emerge.

DIVERGENT PATTERNS OF AGRICULTURE

The reasoning in this chapter and the preceding ones has led up to the conclusion that a small and stagnant population is unlikely to get beyond the stage of primitive agriculture to a higher level of technique and cultural development, while a growing population will be faced with the need to improve the land and perform other investments in agriculture. It is nevertheless likely to experience diminishing returns to labour at least in the short run, and it may have to do longer and harder hours of agricultural work in order to avoid a fall in nutritional standards.

The conclusion would be a dismal one, if this were the whole story. But we have to reckon also with the long-term effects of a gradually increasing population density, and a more favourable picture then emerges. The gradual adaptation to harder and more regular work is likely to raise the efficiency of labour in both agricultural and non-agricultural activities;[2] the increasing density of population opens up opportunities for a more intricate division of labour and—in some cases—a higher degree of urbanization results in improvements in agricultural productivity through the delivery to agriculture of better makes of tool, the provision of better administration, education, etc.

In chapter 2, three broad types of agricultural development were

---

[1] The use of slave raids as a means to avoid agricultural toil is proverbial. A song from ancient Crete gives vivid expression to this idea: 'Ma richesse à moi, c'est une longue lance, une épée, et le beau bouclier qui couvre mon corps. Avec cela je laboure, avec cela je moisonne et je récolte le doux vin de la vigne.' Emile Mireaux, *La vie quotidienne au temps d'Homère* (Paris, 1954), p. 111. In the beginning of this century a member of the Bemba tribe of Rhodesia expressed the same idea by bragging that 'they did not know how to hoe, for their only trade was war'. Audrey I. Richards, op. cit., p. 401.

[2] There are numerous examples of employers in plantations, mines and industries who prefer labourers from regions of intensive agriculture to more unstable labour from regions with less intensive agriculture. See e.g. K. M. Barbour, 'Population, Land and Water in Central Sudan', in Barbour and Prothero, op. cit., p. 142. The author mentions the preference in Sudan for immigrant labourers, who 'come from settled tribes of cultivators, and so they are not afraid of hard work'. Similarly, in various parts of Asia, Chinese labour is preferred to Indian, and Indian to Malay or Burmese labour. There were similar differences in attitude and efficiency among European labourers, related to their agricultural background. In the Soviet Union, the problems of absenteeism, indiscipline and inefficiency were acute in the period when industrial labour had to be recruited among peasant youth accustomed to a highly seasonal rhythm of work.

distinguished. In the two first types, population growth leads to changes in the patterns of land use and in the kind of tools applied, but in one of them, productivity in non-agricultural activities remains at a low level with the result that only primitive makes of tool are used in agriculture despite increasing population and a more and more intensive pattern of land use. By contrast, in the second type of development, the increase in population is accompanied by rising productivity in urban occupations and improvement of the make of agricultural tools so that output per man-hour in agriculture can develop more favourably than in the first type. It is not our concern in this study to investigate the causes of these differences in productivity in non-agricultural activities.

The third kind of development is that of territories where population density has remained very low and the population very poor. This pattern is found in regions with very unfavourable climate and in those communities all over the world which happened to be the victims of slave raids and whose members were thus faced with the alternative of economic and cultural stagnation at home or being absorbed in the conquering and more progressive community at the bottom of its social hierarchy. Likewise within communities where slavery is abolished and where the cultivators have come into contact with advanced civilizations and imported better makes of tool, the members of small ethnic groups tend to remain in isolated groups at a low stage of development, or to be recruited for menial work in neighbouring groups living at higher levels of civilization.

CHAPTER 9

SYSTEMS OF LAND USE AS A
DETERMINANT OF LAND TENURE

The systems of land tenure found in the former European colonies are of a confusing variety, and it is no wonder, therefore, that economists have been inclined to disregard them when they discussed population growth and economic development in underdeveloped countries. It was felt, it seems, that no useful generalizations could be made in this field.

However, we cannot acquiesce with this tradition of treating land tenure as an exogeneous variable, for the observed variations in systems of land tenure—as between countries and as between regions within one and the same country—can to a large extent be explained as the result of two factors: the system of land use in that particular region on one hand and on the other hand the different ways in which the Europeans have adapted the native systems of land tenure, which they found on their arrival, to the requirements of a colonial economy and to their own ideas of how a proper tenure system ought to be.[1] Indeed, the basic pattern which the Europeans found on their arrival in the various parts of the world show a striking co-variance with patterns of land use.

Moreover, the development of land tenure outside Europe—before it came to be tampered with by colonial administrations—seems to be fairly similar to that development of land tenure which we know from historic studies of tenure in Europe.[2] Even pre-Colum-

[1] C. K. Meek, *Land, Law and Custom in the Colonies* (London, 1949). This is a comprehensive study of native tenure systems and of the changes resulting from European influence. Much additional information about this subject is available in *Land Tenure Symposium, Amsterdam*, 1950 (Leiden, 1951); Kenneth H. Parsons *et al.* (ed.), 'Land Tenure', op. cit.; Daniel Biebuyck (ed.), *African Agrarian Systems* (Oxford, 1963).

[2] Alfred Marshall drew attention to this affinity between the European past and the Asian present: 'Modern analysis may be applied to the contemporary conditions of land tenure in India and other Oriental countries ... in such a way as to throw light on the obscure and fragmentary records of medieval land

bian tenure systems in America seem to have had basic features in common with the Old World and with today's underdeveloped regions all over the world. Many apparent differences in land tenure are seen, on closer inspection, to be more verbal than real, stemming from different ways of translating similar concepts into European languages.[1]

Undoubtedly, the similarity of the tenure systems is to be explained by the fact that all native tenure systems are adapted to certain systems of land use and that these have developed along similar lines all over the world, as explained in preceding chapters. The gradual development to more intensive agriculture, under the pressure of increasing populations, was accompanied by a development of land tenure which was basically similar despite local variations in many points of detail. In what follows, an attempt is made to summarize the characteristic features of this process of adaptation of tenure to changes of land use.

Both the physiocrats and the classical economists in Britain based their ideas of the effects of population growth in agriculture upon the assumption that private property in land emerges when agricultural land becomes scarce under the pressure of growing numbers of people. It was assumed, in other words, that agricultural land would remain free for everybody to occupy and use as desired, as long as the population in a given territory was small, but that a class of private landowners would appear as soon as good agricultural land had become scarce.[2]

---

tenures, which may indeed be examined, but cannot be cross-examined.' Marshall, *Principles of Economics*, VI, X, 3.

[1] Ancient Indian land tenure provides an example of the linguistic complexities in cases where both the system of agriculture to be analysed and the language are things of the past. The old texts employ a large number of different words to denote such concepts as cultivated fields and various types of fallow. The situation is similar to that of the African language studied by Pierre de Schlippe (see note 1, page 31); but while the latter could cross-examine the users of the language, this method is not available to the Indian scholars who must remain uncertain about the exact meaning of most of these terms. For certain terms it is even undecided whether they refer to types of land use or to transactions in land. See Sachindra Kumar Maity, *The Economic Life of Northern India in the Gupta Period* (Calcutta, 1957), pp. 23–35.

[2] 'But the land begins to people, and to be cleared more and more. The best lands are in success of time fully occupied. . . . But, at last, every spot has found a master, and those who cannot gain a property therein have no other resource but to exchange the labor of their hands . . . the proprietor . . . is enabled . . . to pay other men to cultivate his land. . . . The proprietor, therefore, might then be eased of the labor of culture, and he soon was so.' Turgot, *Réflexions sur la formation et la distribution des richesses*, paras. 10 and 11. Quoted from the English translation which prefaces the 1801 Basle edition of Adam Smith, *The Wealth of Nations*.

But this is an oversimplification. We have already seen that scarcity of land is a more complex phenomenon than the traditional theory would have us believe. Land may be very scarce from the point of view of a tribe of long-fallow cultivators living in a given territory, while from the point of view of European settlers established in the midst of this same tribal territory land may appear to be in abundant supply. Similarly, the development of rules and customs of land tenure is a much slower and more complicated process than the exponents of the classical theory of land tenure assumed. In fact, it seems that there is never a direct transition from a state where land is free to everybody to one of private property in land for the cultivator or for an absentee landlord.

GENERAL AND SPECIFIC RIGHTS OF CULTIVATION

Virtually all the systems of land tenure found to exist before the emergence of private property in land seem to have this one feature in common: certain families are recognized as having cultivation rights within a given area of land while other families are excluded from such cultivation rights. 'Free' land disappears already before the agricultural stage is reached. Tribes of food collectors and hunters consider that they have exclusive rights to collect food and to hunt in a particular area and when they take to food production the members of such tribes consider that they are the only ones who are entitled to cultivate land in that area.

Under the system of forest fallow, all the members of a tribe dominating a given territory have a general right to cultivate plots of land within the territory, while non-members of the tribe can acquire a right of cultivation only by explicit recognition as 'adopted members' of the tribe. This general right to take part in the cultivation of the land which the group dominates—or imagines to dominate—can never be lost for any member of the cultivator families. They may voluntarily leave the territory for a time, but they can then reclaim their right when they return. Only by being formally expelled from the group itself can a member lose his right of cultivation of land.[1]

In order to understand what happens to tribal tenure under the influence of population growth and shortening of fallow a distinction must be made between the general cultivation right—as described above—and the more specific right a family may have to cultivate a

---

[1] This tribal rule may survive for centuries after the disappearance of the system of tribal tenure. Indians who were expelled from their caste lost their rights in land until in the nineteenth century the British made this illegal.

particular plot of land. Under all systems of fallow a family will retain the exclusive right to the plot it has cleared and cultivated until the harvest has been reaped but it seems to depend upon the pattern of land use in the particular territory for how long a time after the harvesting this exclusive right can still be claimed.

Usually, a family can retain its right to cultivate a given plot throughout the period of fallow, unless this is so long that all traces of previous cultivation is lost. But if, after the lapse of the normal period of fallow, the family does not re-cultivate a given plot, it may lose its right to this particular plot while retaining, of course, the general right to clear a plot within the tribal territory. Thus, the general cultivation right is an inseparable element of the status as member of the tribe and, therefore, in principle inalienable, while the specific right to cultivate an individual plot is lost by desuetude after the lapse of a certain period, the length of which depends upon the system of fallow in that particular territory.

As long as a tribe of forest-fallow cultivators has abundant land at its disposal, a family would have no particular interest in returning to precisely that plot which it cultivated on an earlier occasion. Under these conditions a family which needed to shift to a new plot would simply find a suitable plot, or have it allocated by the chief of the tribe, with no regard to the question of who had formerly cultivated particular plots.

But the situation is apt to change with increasing population, as good plots become somewhat scarce. The cultivators may then wish to begin to recultivate a given plot before the normal period of fallow has elapsed. Under such conditions, a family is likely to become more attached to the plots they have been cultivating on earlier occasions, because it is becoming difficult to find better plots elsewhere which are not already taken up by another family. In other words, the members of the tribe would tend to become more conscious and jealous about their special right to the old plots, and they may hasten to recultivate them lest the cultivation right be forfeited by desuetude.[1]

At this stage, when the attachment of individual families to individual plots becomes more permanent, the custom of pledging land is also likely to emerge. If a family does not need to use a given plot for a certain period it may pledge it to another family which will cultivate it forthwith, but subject to the condition that the land must be returned, upon request, to the former cultivator. This custom of

---

[1] In thirteenth-century Europe a man would lose his right in a forest plot, when the forest became so high 'dass er einem Reiter zu Pferde bis an die Sporen reichte, oder dass ein Paar Ochsen ihn mit dem Joch nicht umdrücken konnten'. K. Bücher, *Die Entstehung der Volkswirtschaft* (Tübingen, 1920), vol. II, p. 37.

pledging is thus a means by which a family can avoid to lose its right to a special plot of land, and it must be distinguished sharply from the sale of land where the former occupier of the land loses all rights in it.

Thus, the attachment of individual families to particular plots becomes more and more important with the gradual shortening of the period of fallow and the reduction of the part of the territory which is not used in the rotation. By the same token, the general right for the members of the tribe to clear a new plot becomes less valuable, because the land which is not reserved fallow land for some family is now likely to be of inferior quality or very difficult to clear. As more and more land is subject to specific cultivation rights little land will be available for redistribution by the chief, and valuable land for re- distribution will become available mainly when a family dies out or leaves the territory. Redistribution of land thus becomes a less important and less frequently exerted function of the chief, and in the end it disappears altogether, although it may continue for many centuries after the cultivation system has changed to that of short fallow.[1]

As long as the general right of cultivation has not lost all its im- portance a sharp social distinction exists in rural communities between cultivator families on one hand and families without cultivation rights on the other, the latter group consisting of strangers, whether they be slaves or free. The members of cultivator families have a right to benefit from the periodic redistributions of land, while strangers with no cultivation rights are, of course, excluded. Hence even those strangers, who are not slaves in a legal sense, are neverthe- less left with no other choice than to do menial work for chiefs or for ordinary members of the dominating tribe.[2] Only those strangers who can subsist by some craft or trade can escape from this destiny.

THE CHARACTERISTICS OF LANDLORD TENURE

In rural communities which have passed beyond the cultivation stage of forest fallow the social hierarchy is not exhaustively characterized

---

[1] In Russia, periodic redistributions of land continued until the twentieth century, while they seem to have ceased in much of western Europe nearly one thousand years earlier. In the folklore of the Indian countryside, there is sufficient reminiscence of this old custom to lend support to the land grant movement of Vinoba Bhave.

[2] Liberated slaves seem to become either labourers or share-croppers, but the distinction between these groups does not seem to be sharp at early stages of development, when they are both remunerated by a share of the harvest they have tilled for the real 'cultivator', i.e. the person with cultivation rights in the village territory. In India, where many old tribal rules have been kept alive, a

by the distinction between families with and families without cultivation rights. Above the group of families with cultivation rights is usually found an upper class of tribal chiefs or feudal landlords, who receive tribute from the cultivators—in kind, in labour or both. In most cases, the feudal landlord class seems to originate from intruding tribes, which establish themselves as ruling groups extracting tribute from the members of the conquered tribe. History knows of many cases where the conquering tribe was of nomadic origin, and there is probably some connection between this subjugation of cultivating tribes by nomads and the process by which forest and bush degenerate into grass land with the result that nomads appear in the region. The emergence of a kind of nobility or aristocracy often seems to follow the introduction of short-fallow cultivation with animal draught power.

We have only sparse information about the emergence of feudal tenures in Europe and other regions of old civilization. But in certain parts of Africa this process is of fairly recent date and therefore less difficult to study. In recent centuries both East and West Africa saw a movement of nomadic tribes from north to south and contacts in various forms developed between these nomadic tribes and the bush-fallow cultivators in the territories they invaded. Some of the nomads established peaceful contacts with the cultivators to whom they sold animal produce against vegetable food and cultivators would arrange for their fields to be manured by the droppings of stationed animals belonging to the nomads.[1] Other nomads, however, in both East and West Africa, established themselves as a feudal government or nobility.[2]

Most students of land tenure systems seem to agree that tribal chiefs are to be regarded as a kind of local government and that the conventional gifts paid to them when they allocate land for cultivation or on other occasions can most conveniently be described as the payment for a public service rather than as rent of land.[3] Following

---

share-cropper is still regarded as ineligible for cultivation rights in the land he has on share, and he is therefore unprotected by the legislation protecting other types of tenants.

[1] See Daryll Forde and Scott, op. cit., pp. 197–211 and p. 171n. See also the chapter on 'The Masai Cattle Herders on the East African Plateau', in C. Daryll Forde, *Habitat, Economy and Society* (London, 1934). The nomads in Africa are hesitant to sell or hire out their animals as draught power for ploughs and other equipment, although they are encouraged to do so by some governments in the countries inhabited by nomadic tribes.

[2] The feudal rule of the Fulani tribe in West Africa is thoroughly analysed in Nadel, op. cit. The feudal tenures in East Africa are discussed in Meek, op. cit., pp. 131–44, and in Jan Vansina, 'Les régimes fonciers Ruanda et Kuba—Une Comparaison', in Biebuyck (ed.), op. cit., pp. 348–60.

[3] 'It cannot be too strongly emphasized that the practice, general all over

Marc Bloch we may consider also feudal aristocracies—at least in the first period of their rule—as government agencies rather than a class of private landowners.[1] The salient features of communities with landlord tenure are best understood, if the rights in land of landlords and overlords are regarded as rights to tax the cultivators.

One of the characteristics of a feudal government is that it operates with little use of money transactions. Taxes are collected and government services of various kinds are provided not by salaried officials, but by local intermediaries between the central government and the people. Such intermediaries are usually of 'noble blood', which means that they belong to the same tribe or ethnic group as the sovereign or overlord. They collect taxes in kind, they may have the right to call up rural youth for labour services and military service and, as a rule, they exert the rights of jurisdiction.

Usually the position of the cultivator with regard to his rights in land does not change because a feudal government imposes itself and levies taxes and labour services. The cultivator families continue to have their hereditary cultivation rights, both general and specific, and redistribution of land by village chiefs may continue without interference from the feudal landlords. Nor does land become alienable by sale; grants of land by overlords to members of the nobility

---

Africa, of paying "tribute" to chiefs in the form of annual gifts of agricultural produce must not be interpreted in terms of "rent" or of "feudalism". The gifts are part of a series of mutual obligations between a chief and his people, of which the right to the undisturbed use of an allotted piece of land is merely incidental.' Meek, op. cit., p. 132. See also p. 24n.

[1] Marc Bloch has stressed the need to distinguish clearly between 'le seigneur' and 'le propriétaire': 'Propriété, propriétaires . . . que, voilà, appliquées au moyen âge, des môts lourdes d'équivoques! La société médiévale ne se caractérisait-elle pas, au contraire, par la coexistence, sur une même fraction du sol, de droits réels concurrents, différents de nature, mais chacun dans sa sphère, également réspectables et tels qu'aucun ne possédait cette plénitude dont l'idée s'attache, dans notre langage, à la notion de propriété?' Marc Bloch, op. cit., vol. II, p. 93. In China, the same idea of 'coexistent' rights in land is expressed by attributing to the landlord the ownership of the land and to the tenant the ownership of the surface or the use of the land. T. H. Shen, op. cit., p. 98. In the quotation which follows, S. F. Nadel points to the complications which appear, when the same term is used to denote the rights of all the 'coexistent' partners in land: 'The village land is administered, that is, held in trust and apportioned—in Nupe terminology "owned"—by the chief. Linguistically the specific character of this administrative right to the disposal of village land is not defined very clearly. The Nupe refer to the chief's control over land in exactly the same terms which they use for the direct utilization and ownership of land by a family head or any individual farmer. The Nupe would use the same term also when speaking of the territory belonging to a village, i.e. the land that is "owned" by the people of the village collectively.' Nadel, op. cit., p. 183. See also Biebuyck (ed.), op. cit., pp. 3 ff.

and others are simply grants of the right to levy taxes, and do not interfere with the hereditary cultivation rights of the peasants. In other words, the beneficiaries of such grants do not become owners of the land in a modern sense.[1]

Now feudal landlords may well use the labour services or hired labourers to clear uncultivated land and set up 'home farms' or manors. These may be regarded as a kind of government farm, and they are comparable to the 'chief's villages', which provided food for the household of African chiefs by means of slave labour, or similar enterprises in the neighbourhood of the ancient city states. It is pointless to ask whether these manors or these 'chief's villages' belong to the landlord in his public or private capacity, since the very distinction between a public and a private sphere implied in this question is alien to the feudal society, at least in its early stages.

But not all the land of 'home farms' is acquired by the clearing of hitherto uncultivated land in the manner just described. In communities under landlord tenure a gradual transfer of cultivation rights from the peasants to the landlords may take place. The landlord will often have the power to prevent the redistribution of vacant land by claiming that he is the rightful heir to peasant families who die out or leave the village. Thus, land is added to the 'home farm', to be cultivated by labourers or share-croppers.

Another procedure is for the landlord to abolish the villagers' right to clear plots for cultivation in the forests. The motivation for this attack on the villagers' customary rights may be to make it impossible for the peasants to subsist by means of uncontrolled and untaxed cultivation in the forest and thus place before them the choice between cultivation of village land, for which they must pay taxes, or the acceptance of wage labour for the landlord. It follows that restrictions on the use of forest land may be imposed in periods when labour, not land, is in short supply, but such measures by which the landlord encroaches upon the villagers' rights in land tend to become more frequent when increasing population pressure makes all kinds of land—arable, grazing and forest land—more scarce, and such encroachment very profitable for the landlord.

The preceding description of broad tendencies simplifies the picture which meets us when we look at particular rural communities.

[1] 'In the theory of Nizam ul-Mulk the rights of the muqta' over the population in his igta' were only financial. He had no rights over the land or the cultivators, the ruler merely having delegated to him certain financial rights.' Ann K. S. Lambton, *Landlord and Peasant in Persia* (London, 1953), p. 66. 'The fiefs they granted (in Northern Nigeria) were in effect administrative areas, and the right of the fief-holder to take a share of the tax collected was a reward for political or military services. To this extent the system resembled that of the Mogul empire in India.' Lord Hailey, op. cit., p. 788.

It was shown in chapter 6 that different types of land use may coexist for centuries or more in one and the same district or village territory. By the same token, different systems of tenure come to coexist. It may be, for instance, that part of the land in a village, which is under intensive types of land utilization, is under the permanent cultivations right of particular families, or such land may have become the private property of these families, while land under more extensive systems of land use is still at free disposal for cultivation by any family with general cultivation rights in the village. Such coexistence of tenure systems is known from the agrarian history of Europe, and it is found in underdeveloped countries all over the world.[1]

GRAZING RIGHTS AND SHORTENING OF FALLOW PERIODS

Under both long- and short-fallow systems the land lying fallow at any given time is at the free disposal for grazing by domestic animals belonging to families with cultivation rights, and normally no attempt is made to distinguish between animals and plots or fields belonging to individual families. Even with short fallow and annual cropping, where a family cultivates the same plots year after year, the fields may continue to be available for free grazing by the animals belonging to the whole group of local cultivators during the period from harvest until the preparation of the field for the next crop. However, when grazing opportunities become scarce, rules are likely to be laid down concerning the number of animals a cultivator family is allowed to have and the amount of straw the cultivator is allowed to remove with the harvest. The techniques of harvesting sometimes reflect the exigencies of such rules. In France, the scythe was not allowed to replace the sickle as long as the communal right to feed animals on the stubble continued to exist.[2]

The grazing rights may prevent or delay progress not only with respect to harvest tools but also in the use of land. A cultivator who wishes to introduce a new method of cultivation, with a shorter period of fallow, may be prevented from doing so because it would be an infringement on other cultivators' right to graze their animals on his fallow land. The grazing rights may delay also the change-over to feeding with cultivated fodder plants, because an individual cultivator who desires to introduce this innovation would have to carry the full

---

[1] The Ottoman system of land tenure seems to be essentially a codification of such a mixed system. A description of this tenure system in its relation to various types of land use in regions of previous French Africa is given in Land Tenure Symposium, op. cit.

[2] In Java, it is a strict rule, sanctioned by religious ideas, that the rice plant must be cut with a small knife immediately below the ears.

burden of producing the fodder and feeding it to the animals while benefit of reduced pressure on the communal grazing land accrues to the other cultivators.[1]

It is no wonder, then, that the problem of grazing rights comes to the fore at a certain stage of population density and contributes to create tension between the cultivators and the feudal landlord about the rights to use the uncultivated land surrounding the villages. This problem is usually a major political issue in the late feudal period.

The cultivators' communal rights to use fallow land for grazing will usually survive long after the general right to clear new forest land has disappeared. In western Europe the communal grazing right in fallow did not disappear before the period when the short-fallow system was replaced by annual cropping and in many other parts of the world common grazing of harvested fields continue even where one or two crops are taken every year.

FROM LANDLORD TENURE TO PRIVATE PROPERTY IN LAND

The gradual disappearance of the general rights to clear new plots and to graze the animals freely in fallow and commons and the replacement of these rights by the permanent right of each cultivator family over particular pieces of land, is only one link in the chain of events which gradually changes the agrarian structure in such a way that private property in land becomes a dominating feature. Another sequence of change is connected with the gradual penetration of money transactions to the villages, a process which is of course connected with the degree of urbanization.

Apart from localities through which a road of transit trade is passing and from open economies of the colonial type, money payments are likely to play only a marginal role in the villages before the stage of short fallow is reached. In villages distant from urban centres, money payments may be absent even at stages of annual and multi-cropping. In such cases the central government continues to rely on local landlords as intermediaries for the collection of taxes in kind and for the organization of public works as labour service.

The process by which the feudal landlord tenure is abandoned may take different forms: sometimes the position of the feudal landlords in relation to the cultivators is weakened; they lose their power over all or most of the peasants and they end up as private owners of their home farms only. In other cases, the feudal landlords succeed in their efforts to completely eliminate the customary rights of the cultivators and they end as private owners of all the land over which they had

[1] See note 1, page 37.

feudal rights, whilst the cultivators have sunk to the status of tenants-at-will.[1]

England, of course, is the classical example of this last kind of development. The completeness with which the feudal lords were transformed into private owners, with the cultivators as tenants, is reflected in the fact that modern English fails to distinguish between a feudal landlord and a modern owner of real estate: they are both 'landlords'. The traditional economic concept of land tenure mentioned at the beginning of this chapter is a reflection of the arguments upon which the French and English feudal landlords based their case, pointing to the precedent of Roman law.[2] The hereditary cultivation rights of the peasants are ignored and land is considered as a free resource where there is no 'scarcity of land' and elsewhere as the private property of the landlord. He can claim a rent which is determined not by custom but by the market, and, if he pleases, he can evict the peasants.

This concept of land tenure barred the way to an understanding of the dynamics of land tenure as determined primarily by changes in methods of cultivation.

The use of the term 'landlord' for two widely different economic functions can help to explain the misunderstanding of British colonial administrators without insight in tribal and feudal tenure systems. They treated both tribal chiefs and feudal lords as if they were private landowners without any public functions. Even today one may find statements in economic literature about landlords, for instance in the Middle East, who 'own hundreds of villages'. The truth is, of course, that they have 'seigneurial rights' over them; they are 'seigneurs', but not 'propriétaires'. In cases where it is impossible to overlook the fact that feudal landlords have certain public functions and are not landowners in the modern sense the appropriate term 'landlord' is often avoided and replaced by misleading ones like 'warlords', 'generals' or 'revenue farmers'.

[1] In Persia, this process seems to have taken place as late as the twentieth century: 'The general trend of events since the grant of the Constitution in 1906 . . . has been in fact to alter the status of the large landed proprietor from that of a petty territorial prince to that of an ordinary landowner. The change has not been . . . an abrupt one: it began in the early Constitutional period, and culminated in the reign of Riza Shah.' Lambton, op. cit., p. 260. See also ibid., pp. 330–1.

[2] Marc Bloch, op. cit., vol. I, pp. 189–90.

CHAPTER 10

INVESTMENT AND TENURE IN TRIBAL COMMUNITIES

In all communities, apart from the most primitive ones, a high rate of population growth necessitates a high rate of investment. It is often suggested in the literature on the economic problems of pre-industrial countries that income per head is so low that overall saving in the community cannot be sustained at a level sufficiently high to finance the investment which is necessary if a high rate of population growth is to be compatible with constant or even rising incomes per head.

This general problem of the financing of investment in under-developed countries is not our concern in this study. We are interested more particularly in the problems of agricultural investment and saving during periods of growing population. The first important thing to note about agricultural investment is that a large share of it can be carried out by the cultivators themselves. Furthermore, it is normal for cultivators to have shorter or longer periods of leisure each year when current agricultural work is at a minimum so that working capacity for additional investment is normally available. In other words, the question is not whether the cultivators are able and willing to restrain consumption in order to invest. The question is whether an increasing family provides sufficient incentive to ad-ditional work and whether the system of land tenure is such that the cultivators have access to additional cultivable land or sufficient security of tenure to make land improvements a worthwhile investment.

It was seen in the preceding chapters that both the nature of the needed investment, the amount of off-season leisure and the system of land tenure are apt to undergo important changes when one system of land use is substituted for another. It is futile, therefore, to seek a universally valid explanation of how a rise of the rate of population growth affects investment and savings in rural communities. The analysis will have to be carried out separately for each system of land use and tenure. For the sake of brevity, only three typical stages will be discussed here:

(*a*) There is first the type of community in which long-fallow cultivators, in order to cope with increasing population, must do additional land clearing or make land improvements for the change-over to more intensive systems of land use. The relevant assumption about land tenure in this type of community is that the general right of cultivation is still in force and that the specific rights to cultivate particular plots have not yet resulted in a situation where all families permanently occupy individual plots.

(*b*) The next type to be considered is the settled peasant community where growing populations must create additional arable fields for short-fallow cultivation or invest in other types of land improvement in order to be able to crop existing arable land more frequently. In this case the relevant assumption about land tenure is that a cultivator family permanently occupies given plots of arable land, but as a hereditary cultivation right subject to feudal authority and taxation.

(*c*) The third stage to be discussed is that where modern tenure predominates and where most of the cultivators own the land and pay with money for agricultural labour and for the purchase of non-agricultural consumer goods, while they continue to use little or no industrial input in agriculture.

The present chapter is devoted to a discussion of investment problems in the first of these three types of community while chapters 11 and 12 deal with the two other stages. Some problems arising from the use of industrial input in primitive agriculture will be briefly dealt with in chapter 13.

ORGANIZATION OF INVESTMENT UNDER TRIBAL TENURE

In very primitive communities of long-fallow cultivation where a given plot is cultivated for only one or two seasons and where the huts are frequently removed and rebuilt the very distinction between investment activity and current work is questionable. When capital is very short-lived the amount of investment per inhabitant must be virtually the same regardless of the rate at which population is growing. Under tribal organization most land clearing is done by the young men of the tribe working in common, and it is in the interest of the whole tribe that a large number of male children should grow up to the age where they can undertake clearing work. In such communities rapid population growth creates no difficulty with clearing of land, but it may create problems of exhaustion of land and erosion, as already mentioned.

If population in long-fallow communities becomes so dense that the periods of cultivation must be prolonged, the superficial clearing of a relatively large area is replaced by a far more thorough clearing of a fraction of the area each year. The total amount of clearing work to be performed annually by a population of given size is likely to be roughly similar in the two cases, but because the investment period has become longer the amount of annual clearing work per head must vary significantly with changes in the rate of growth of population. It is unlikely, nevertheless, that the availability of labour for doing the annual clearing work would be a limiting factor, even with a rapid acceleration of the rate of population growth, as long as clearing is done by means of fire. Many tribal populations have a large share of their young men absent from the tribe for years, performing labour service or wage labour in mines, plantations and towns, but the necessary clearing work nevertheless gets done by those who remain. If the young men remain at home and the system of tribal co-operation continues to function, there is little doubt that long-fallow communities can cope with the investments needed for increasing rates of population growth.

It has been mentioned that in the past many growing tribes preferred to use their young men in warfare and to let the captives in these wars and their off-spring do the hard work at home. A large part of the investment work in rapidly growing tribes was probably made by slave labour. Not only clearing of land may have been done in this way, but also land improvements necessary in the change-over from long-fallow to plough cultivation or from long-fallow to intensive cultivation of irrigated terraces.

When regions of long-fallow cultivation came under European influence, the conditions for investment activity often changed, partly because the slaves were exported or slavery abolished while labour-services and non-agricultural wage labour was introduced, and partly because the Europeans introduced changes in land tenure. In some cases the Europeans confiscated tribal land for their own use; in other cases the advent of the Europeans had the effect to bar the free access to tribal land for the members of a tribe because the claim of a tribal chief, or of somebody else, to be owner ef the land might get the support of the foreigners. Most colonial administrations started out with the preconceived idea that it was in the interest of everybody that private property in land should be introduced as quickly as possible, and often self-interest and convenience made them recognize either Europeans or tribal chiefs as full-fledged owners of large areas of tribal land. Ordinary members of the tribes, who did not want to become wage labourers or tenants for the new owners had to migrate either to towns, mines and plantations, or to less densely peopled regions.

90

When tribal chiefs manage to be confirmed as private owners of tribal land a breakdown of the whole tribal organization of investment may ensue, because the young men may then refuse to do the clearing as free service for the tribal community. In other cases, the first step towards a breakdown of tribal solidarity comes from the young men themselves. Through their work for the Europeans and in other ways the young men of the tribe come under the influence of individualistic attitudes to work and remuneration, and as a consequence they may refuse to do unpaid clearing work for the tribe as a whole and insist on having privately owned plots in the tribal area instead of being subject to the authority of the chief.[1] Where this happens, the tribal chief becomes the defender of the customary tenure against modernizing elements of the native population. The Europeans will then be found supporting one side or other, depending on their own interest or on the general attitude of the colonial officer in charge or of his home government.

CONTEST OVER PROPERTY RIGHTS

The individualistic attitudes are most pronounced in those tribal regions of Asia and Africa, where missionaries, mining companies or plantations have created opportunities of contact with Europeans and introduced western-type education. Such regions are also those where medical and sanitary progress first contributed to reduce mortality and increase the rate of natural population growth. Moreover, these regions where a certain degree of urbanization has been reached are apt to attract immigrants from tribal regions which are less densely populated. Thus, the tribal regions where population is growing most rapidly are those where contacts with Europeans over long periods have created various types of 'mixed tenure', or at least created an awareness of the existence of European types of tenure.

A sustained and rapid increase of population must end by creating the need for land improvements as a pre-condition for the transition to systems of shorter periods of fallow or no fallow at all. In the regions where the influence of western attitudes has been strong none of the old communal ways of organizing such investments are possible today. Those who wish, under the western influence, to break away from the traditional pattern will seek to introduce private ownership of land in order to create security for individual investments, and this may create problems with already established feudal

---

[1] The effects of European influence on tribal organization in Africa are discussed in Georges Balandier, *Sociologie actuelle de l'Afrique noire* (Paris, 1955). See especially pp. 209–18, 258–70 and 364–6; Lord Hailey, op. cit., pp. 775–815; Meek, op. cit., *passim*; Land Tenure Symposium, op. cit., see especially p. 98 and Biebuyck (ed.), op. cit., *passim*.

landlords or with nomadic tribes, who want to reserve grazing land as private or tribal property. But these are not the only problems or even the most difficult ones. The greatest difficulty lies in the conflicts among the cultivators themselves which are inevitable as soon as private ownership of land emerges in communities which continue to apply long-fallow systems.

Such conflicts among the cultivators are likely to appear when natural population growth or concentration of population near urban centres has been so rapid that the problem of ownership of land has presented itself while the general right to clearing of plots in common land is still a living reality and before the individual cultivator families have got permanent attachment to particular plots of land. If gradual shortening of fallow has led a cultivator family to cultivate the same land for many generations, there is little doubt about the land distribution among the cultivator families, only the problem of elimination of feudal intermediaries may be at issue. But where the cultivator families are still moving their cultivation from one plot to another, or did so until recently, it may be impossible even for the disinterested expert to disentangle the property rights in a given plot.

The difficulty of the problem should be apparent from what was said in the preceding chapter about the difference between the general right to clear plots, which is unlimited in time, and the special right to a particular plot which is limited in time, but may be kept alive by pledging. Such pledging may be difficult to distinguish from modern lease on one hand and sale of land on the other.[1] In communities where all these types coexist and some or all of the partners in transactions concerning land are illiterate and have many different ideas of the type of contracts they are making, the inevitable result is a confused legal situation which is difficult to handle for the honest judge and easy to misuse for the most clever among the partners to the transactions.

In communities of this type each new step on the road to private property in land may well create less and not more security of tenure, and a vast amount of litigation is the obvious result. Litigation accompanied attempts to introduce private property in land in ancient Rome and the same happened during European colonization

---

[1] 'The letting out of land is discountenanced, although this practice is considered to be less objectionable to established custom if the rent takes the form of a share of the produce, thus bringing the transaction within the convention of a partnership in cultivation.' Lord Hailey, op. cit., p. 803. 'Native landowners (in Kenya E.B.) are generally averse to receiving regular rent, since this might be interpreted as pledging their interest in the land.' Meek, op. cit., p. 98. Nadel deals with the same problem (op. cit., pp. 192–5). See also A. J. Köbben, 'Land as an Object of Gain in a Non-Literate Society, Land-Tenure among the Bete and Dida (Ivory Coast, West Africa)', in Biebuyck (ed.), op. cit., pp. 257–9.

of Asia, Latin America and Africa.[1] Also after the previous colonies have become independent, clever individuals or groups make attempts to become legal owners of land over which others have customary rights of cultivation. The latter lose their security of tenure and the former may not obtain real security, because new litigation may end in reversal of the previous decision.[2]

In some cases the partners in the contest about land are tribal chiefs against their own members or enterprising members of a tribe against their fellow tribesmen, with the tribal chiefs loyally defending the interests of the latter. In other cases, the partners belong to different tribes or the contest is between members of a tribe and more advanced 'non-tribal' elements of the population. In such cases the issue may give rise to a communal strife between ethnic groups.

Colonial governments sometimes saw their interest in protecting the tribes against the national majority or the weaker tribes against the stronger ones as part of the principle of 'divide and rule'. After independence the minority groups have lost this protection and sometimes they are left with only the choice between seeing their rights in land impaired by the growing rural population belonging to the majority groups or taking illegal action to protect them. Such questions of changes in land use because of growing numbers in both majority and minority groups are behind much communal strife in former colonies and contributed to lend passion to some of the civil wars of the post-war period. The problem has come to the fore primarily in Asia and Africa, but is latent in parts of Latin America too.[3]

Rapid population increase in regions of long-fallow cultivation may cause strife about land tenure and sometimes serious soil erosion, but the positive effects of rapid population growth in such regions should not be overlooked. The most serious deterrent to economic development in sparsely populated regions is the burden of

[1] J. S. Furnivall, op. cit., pp. 134–7 (litigation in Burma); E. H. Jacoby, *Agrarian Unrest in South-East Asia* (1949), p. 180 (litigation in the Philippines); Francisco Ponce de Léon, 'The Problem of Land Ownership in Peru', in Kenneth H. Parsons, op. cit., p. 271 (litigation in Peru); T. Olawale Elias, *Nigerian Land Law and Custom* (London, 1953), especially pp. 257–8 and 301 (litigation in Nigeria); Georges Balandier, op. cit., p. 365 (litigation in the Congo); Meek, op. cit., pp. 169 ff. (litigation in Ghana); Lambton, op. cit., p. 289 (registration of land followed by litigation in tribal areas of Persia).

[2] C. K. Meek mentions that people postpone their legal claims in land until the possessor has made extensive land improvements. Meek, op. cit., p. 25.

[3] 'The conflicts arising from the claims of the Indian communities in Peru on the best right of ownership of cultivated and pasture lands, constitute one of the most acute manifestations of the so-called Indian problem, whose causes rather than being of a racial nature assume a demographic, economic, social and cultural aspect.' Alberto Arca-Parró, 'Land Tenure Problems Rooted in the Ethnic History of Latin America', in Kenneth H. Parsons, op. cit., p. 282.

public investments, which a sparse and poor population is unable to shoulder without assistance from outside. It is true of many kinds of public investment that they are determined by the size of the area more than by the number of inhabitants. An increase of population reduces the per capita costs of such investments and services in rural areas, and this advantage is likely to be so large that it can more than offset the relatively light burden of some additional agricultural investment. For this reason, even rapid and prolonged population increase in tribal regions seems more likely to be a blessing than a curse, if the political problems connected with land tenure and the technical problems connected with prevention of soil erosion can be solved.[1]

[1] The East Africa Royal Commission of 1953–5 concluded that 'given the necessary economic and social changes, an increase in population might actually contribute to a rise in the general standard of life'. Lord Hailey, op. cit., p. 1355.

CHAPTER 11

RURAL INVESTMENT UNDER
LANDLORD TENURE

As explained in previous chapters, communities with landlord tenure often have systems of cultivation with a highly seasonal pattern of agricultural employment. Except for periods when the soil is frozen, the off-season periods can normally be used for investment activities, and this facilitates the creation of additional fields, minor irrigation works and other kinds of investment which can be performed by the cultivators in the immediate neighbourhood of their villages with the tools they normally use in their current work. Thus the essential pre-condition for this type of investment activity to be undertaken is that rural population increase provides hands enough to cultivate more land or reap more crops from a given area.

It might be objected, perhaps, that such investment could be prevented by the landlords. It seems unlikely, however, that the necessary expansion of food production would be thwarted by a restrictionist cultivation policy by landlords. It is true, of course, that once the landlords have abolished the general right to clear plots in uncultivated land, the cultivators must ask his permission to take additional land under cultivation. But in periods of rapid population growth the feudal lords must have every interest in seeing the young peasants settled. It is true of virtually all of the agricultural taxes and services due to the feudal landlord that their proceeds are roughly in proportion to the number of peasant families under his jurisdiction. The more peasants become settled in the villages over which he dominates and the more new villages he can create the greater will be the revenue accruing to the landlord and his overlord.

In order to raise the number of revenue-paying peasant households under their domination, feudal landlords and overlords in all parts of the world have organized the clearing of forests, draining of swamps and building of villages whenever the increase of population made it possible to create new agricultural units. European kings were particularly eager to settle peasant sons, when they were in financial difficulties and needed additional sources of revenue. Often much of the investment was made by means of labour service, so that the peasant youth were themselves doing the investment. When the investments were finished, they would be settled on the land which they had themselves cleared and improved.

But neither feudal landlords nor kings can wish to settle all rural youth. Besides revenue, they need servants, bodyguards and soldiers, and these requirements set an upper limit to the investment activity in agriculture they are willing to organize. The lower limit is set by labour productivity in agriculture. If the lord adds too lavishly to the number of servants and the king requests too large numbers of soldiers those left behind in agricultural pursuits may be too few to feed the excessive numbers of people outside agriculture. Stocks are reduced both with the peasants and elsewhere, and when a harvest failure occurs the result is famine. Harvest failures, as already mentioned, are frequent under a short-fallow cultivation which must rely on rain-fed mono-cropping of cereals.

It is widely believed that famines in rural communities under feudal tenure stem from over-population of the land, the explanation being that the rules of feudal tenure are a disincentive to the intensification of agriculture. Quite contrary to this view, I find it more likely that famines would occur in communities under feudal tenure as a result of rural underpopulation relative to total population and to agricultural productivity. Feudal landlords and governments are likely to reduce the village population too much in their desire for soldiers, servants and luxuries and by their related attempt to tax the peasants heavily. Too little food is then produced and too much of it removed from the villages, which are left without stocks of food to help them in years of bad harvest.

The idea that famines bear witness to rural overpopulation is largely an inference from the commonly observed phenomenon of rural underemployment. As already explained, however, this underemployment in villages under feudal tenure is primarily of a seasonal kind, and it seems utterly unlikely that feudal landlords would allow any considerable number of able-bodied persons to remain underemployed in the village if they could be spared in the peak season.[1]

INTENSIVE AGRICULTURE WITH FEUDAL LANDLORDS

In regions with a less humid climate than western Europe, feudal

---

[1] 'La préoccupation principale est d'installer tout le monde au travail, de ne tolérer aucun parasite. Le seigneur n'a jamais trop de serviteurs.' A. Sauvy, op. cit., vol. I (Paris, 1952), p. 138.

organizations may derive a large share of their revenue from the taxation of water for irrigation, and it may be asked how such taxation—which usually consists of a share in all crops grown on irrigated land—is likely to influence agricultural land use. It is well known that under modern systems of agriculture share-cropping arrangements are apt to discourage the intensification of agricultural production. It is unwarranted, however, to infer that share-cropping with high crop-shares paid for irrigated land is likewise an obstacle under feudal conditions, where the peasant is not free to decide whether he wants to irrigate or not. If the landlord constructs canals to provide the field with water, the peasant must pay the high crop-share for irrigated crops and he must use the water in order to be able to pay. The crucial question, therefore, concerns the landlord's incentive to organize investments in irrigation work rather than the peasant's incentive to use the facilities.

The water rate which the feudal landlord can impose on the peasant is not the only benefit he derives from the provision of irrigation facilities. Irrigated land produces both larger and more frequent crops than unirrigated land, and ordinary tax revenue from the land which is normally in direct proportion to the harvest, must therefore increase as a result of the irrigation works undertaken by the landlord. By providing irrigation a landlord can usually obtain a larger share of a larger harvest once or twice a year instead of a relatively small share of a small harvest every second or third year. There is, therefore, little reason to doubt that he will call up the peasants for the construction of irrigation facilities as soon as the increase of the village population makes it possible for them to produce and handle larger and more frequent harvests than hitherto.[1]

If the feudal crop-share to the landlord is raised, because water is provided, the peasant does not necessarily become poorer. It is more likely that his net income will increase because he will get a smaller share of much larger harvests. However, he will normally have to work many more hours per year with irrigated crops than he did with dry ones, as discussed in chapter 5, and he is likely to resent this reduction of his customary seasonal leisure. Active feudal régimes are often accused of an oppressive policy towards the peasants because, in periods of rising population, they force them to undertake land improvements and work hard in order to pay high crop-shares.[2]

In fact, it is a valid generalization to say that in feudal economies the most prosperous periods are those when population is rising rapidly, and much land clearing, irrigation and terracing of hillsides

[1] In an ancient Indian text, the *Kamandaka*, the construction of dams across rivers and the peopling of uninhabited tracts were mentioned as two of the eight sources of revenue. See Maity, op. cit., p. 55.

[2] The Mogul reign in India seems to provide an example of this. In modern

is going on. In periods of rapid population increase, the desire for additional soldiers and luxuries can, more easily than in periods of stagnant population, be satisfied without depopulation of the villages and neglect of agriculture. In other words, population growth often seems to be the cause of prosperity, in sharp contrast to the causation from prosperity to population growth and poverty, which was suggested by Malthus.

THE NEGLECT OF INVESTMENT UNDER COLONIAL RULE

As already said, feudal landlord tenure may be regarded as a type of government organization, superimposed on the remnants of the tribal tenure system. Three main cases can be distinguished with regard to the conditions for agricultural investment under this type of tenure:

(a) The overlord or central government is in a strong position and can effectively control that the local landlords perform their public duties. If necessary, the central government will devote part of its own revenue to agricultural investment and rural services in supplement to those financed by the local landlords.

(b) A strong overlord or central government effectively controls not only that the landlords levy taxes, but also that they pass most of them on to the central authority, which uses this revenue largely for military expense or for urban luxuries. This policy by the central authority is not incompatible with the development of the urban economy, but it is obviously inimical to agricultural investment and tends to result in rural depopulation.

(c) The overlord or central government is weak and has no effective control over the landlords. These are passively allowed to neglect their public duties, without their functions being taken over by the central authority.

European colonial administrations mostly belonged to the third of these categories. This could sometimes be explained by the long distances from mother country to colony, as in the case of the Spanish Government which failed to control the Spanish feudal landlord class in Latin America. In other cases, colonial administrations deliberately refrained from controlling the non-European feudal land-

---

Indian literature, the oppressiveness of this regime is often illustrated by reference to the raising of crop-shares from one-sixth under the ancient Hindu kingdoms to one-third or one-half under the Moguls. However, sources dating from the first millennium A.D. mention crop-shares ranging from one-sixth for barren and rocky land to one-half for land under river irrigation (Maity, op. cit., p. 56). When river irrigation spread under the Moguls, the higher shares would have become more frequent, even where customary rates for land of a given quality were unchanged.

lords in colonies and other dependencies, because they wished, foi political reasons, to be on good terms with the local ruling class in the colony. French administrations in parts of North Africa and English in parts of India are examples.[1] Such a policy was possible, because most government revenue came from sources other than indigenous agriculture and because food could be imported from other colonies, if neglect of local agriculture led to shortages.

It did not matter so much to western European agriculture if governments failed to control the feudal landlords, because agricultural investments in the feudal and late feudal periods in western Europe were mainly of the type which the peasant families could carry out themselves, if necessary. It is more serious when feudal landlords fail to perform their normal functions in regions dependent on large-scale irrigation, such as parts of North African and Asian agriculture, as well as the agriculture of some pre-Colombian civilizations in America.

When such regions are left in the uncontrolled possession of a landlord class, which is either of foreign origin or partner in a precarious alliance with a foreign conqueror, rural investments are in danger of being neglected, because the landlords inevitably go for quick profits and liquid assets. In extreme cases, the result is starvation and depopulation as seems to have occurred on a large scale in Latin America.[2] In other cases, the population continues to grow, but underemployment ensues and emigration follows in its wake, because investment is insufficient for an expansion of agricultural output and employment. When European administrations prohibited the use of labour services, without an abolition of the landlord system as such, rural investment could hardly avoid to be affected. Such regions of neglected irrigation are often held forth as standard examples of the disastrous results of population growth, without due examination of the special causes of the plight of local agriculture.

The classical example of colonial interference with indigenous tenures is that of British India. Land tenure in the paddy producing regions of India, which had been under Mogul rule, were of the usual

[1] Uganda is another example. Cf. the following comments on the results of the granting of proprietary rights to the feudal fief-holders in the beginning of the twentieth century: 'The holding of land has in effect been divorced from the exercise of those political functions on which the control over land had previously depended, so that the relation of landlord and tenant is now purely commercial.' Lord Hailey, op. cit., p. 787.

[2] It has been suggested that the depopulation of the previous Inca empire can be explained in part by the fact that the Spanish landlords transferred manpower to non-agricultural activities, such as mining, manufacturing of textiles and cultivation of cocoa, with the result that the production of basic food was neglected. Alberto Arca-Parró, op. cit., in Kenneth H. Parsons. op. cit., pp. 277–83.

feudal type with very high dues. The British conquerors began by giving the feudal landlords the same status as landlords in England had obtained; later this policy had to be revised and replaced by a tenancy legislation with regulated rents to be paid in money, and with the re-establishment of hereditary cultivation rights for the peasants. Increase of agricultural prices during the colonial period reduced the real value of the controlled rents with the result that the landlords lost both the incentive and the means to invest in water control.

Also in this case the effects of the disorganization of the feudal system was quite different from the effects of similar changes in Europe, because the needed investments were of another type. The protected tenants in India had no organization to undertake comprehensive water control schemes, and the whole system of legally frozen tenures was an obstacle also to small-scale investment in agriculture. Thus disorganization of the feudal system contributed to prevent agricultural output from responding to population increase in the colonial period, and the feudal tenures had to be abolished before federal and state governments of independent India and Pakistan could take steps in the direction of a more intensive pattern of land use.

THE RESPONSE TO PRICE INCENTIVES

Many experts of land tenure and economists dealing with problems of pre-industrial agriculture consider that the rules of feudal tenure are obstacles to investment and thus contribute to create underemployment in agriculture in periods of rapid population growth. The preceding discussion suggests that feudal tenure is not in all cases an obstacle to agricultural investment. If the feudal organization is left intact, it is likely to absorb all rural population surpluses in either non-agricultural or agricultural employment, at least as far as the peak seasons of agricultural work are concerned.

There are exceptions to this rule, however. Both feudal and tribal tenure systems may stand in the way of intensification of agriculture. It was seen that they are most likely to do so when the feudal system becomes disorganized in regions depending on large-scale irrigation; other examples, well known from Europe's agrarian history, are that of strip farming preventing the elimination of fallow, and that of common grazing rights hindering the introduction of cultivated fodder plants. However, such obstacles provided by land tenure are sometimes swept away when economic incentives to intensification become strong. We saw it in parts of western Europe where the feudal landlords were the ones who took the initiative for the abolition of feudalism because prices had become attractive to intensive land use as a result of rapid growth of population and increasing urbanization.[1]

If feudal tenures exist in regions where increasing rural populations are unable to find sufficient employment because of the survival of extensive forms of land use, it is often suggested as an explanation that the feudal landlords are behaving uneconomically, showing more interest in the prestige of land ownership than in the profits of intensive agriculture.

I wonder whether this theory of a strongly traditional attitude of feudal landlords has any firm foundation. When overall population growth promotes intensive land use and a change of the system of tenure in regions close to expanding urban centres, extensive land use is likely to continue to be more profitable than intensive in regions far from large urban centres. Feudal landlords in such regions may well be behaving economically when they refuse to change both land use and tenure, and it seems to me more pertinent to regard the rural migration which accompanies such divergent trends in land use and tenure as a necessary concomitant of the concentration of non-agricultural activities in particular regions, rather than to interpret it as the result of non-economic behaviour by feudal landlords.

---

[1] For a discussion of the interrelationship between developments of land tenure in the late feudal period and the process of industrialization in Europe and Asia, see M. Boserup, 'Agrarian Structure and Take-off', in W. W. Rostow (ed.), *The Economics of Take-off into Sustained Growth* (London, 1963), pp. 201–24.

CHAPTER 12

INCENTIVES TO INVESTMENT UNDER MODERN TENURE

The previous chapters were concerned with the effects of population increase on investment in agriculture under systems of tribal and feudal tenure. This leaves us with the problem of the effects of population increase on agricultural investment in pre-industrial societies under modern tenure   where the cultivators own their land or rent it from private landowners against rent in money or in kind.

In rural communities at this stage, rent, wages and taxes may be paid either in money or in kind and in many cases cultivators' and labourers' money purchases of consumer goods are considerable. However, the rural economy is still far from being a money economy in any full sense of the word, as long as purchases of industrial input for agriculture are insignificant and the peasants produce a relatively large share of their own food consumption. As long as the economy to which the rural communities belong is at a low stage of industrialization, agriculture is unlikely to use more than insignificant amounts of industrial input and nearly all private investment in agriculture is likely to be done by local labour with traditional tools.[1] However,

[1] Economists from industrialized countries are prone to under-estimate the amount of investment made by the peasants themselves in this type of community during periods of rising population. For instance, in an important and well-known study of the economic problem of population growth in India, it was assumed that this type of 'non-monetized' investment consists mainly of rural housing and would be likely to decline in the decade 1960 to 1970, in spite of the rapid growth of population. See Ansley J. Coale and Edgar M. Hoover, *Population Growth and Economic Development in Low Income Countries* (Princeton, 1958), pp. 235–6. In recent years, however, the importance of this type of investment has come to be more fully recognized in India. (See, for instance, the paper by Mahaviar Prasad, Irrigation Adviser to the Government of India, 'Problems of Irrigation and Water Use in India'. Paper presented to the United Nations Conference, op. cit., agenda item C.3.2.) The disturbingly low rate of utilization of new irrigation facilities constructed by public authorities is now generally ascribed to the failure of the cultivators to provide their share of the investment effort in the shape of feeder canals and other 'non-monetized' investment.

the organization of large-scale investment in irrigation, etc., has become a matter for central or local governments to deal with, and such investment is carried out with wage labour, but usually with little or no modern industrial equipment.[1]

Let us assume that the government takes the initiative to the large scale investments which are needed for the expansion of agricultural production as population increases, and that they recruit the labourers in the rural labour market and finance the works by taxes levied on the cultivators, so that the urban sector makes no contribution to the financing of this rural investment.

Under such conditions, the share of the rural population working in the farms is reduced when the rate of population growth increases, because rural workers must be recruited for public investments. Those left in the farms must do added work per head in order to pay the higher taxes and to take care of the increase in private investment in agriculture which is made necessary by the increase in the rate of population growth. The main question is whether the agriculturists are willing and able to prolong their work-hours sufficiently to do this.

The statement that an increase of the rate of population growth must create an additional work burden per head rather than additional underemployment is in sharp contrast to what is generally taken for granted in modern discussions of the subject, which are mostly based upon the tacit assumption that neither the government nor the cultivators would make any attempt to undertake the investment that is necessary to cope with the increased rate of population growth or that such investment must necessarily be done with mechanized equipment and little use of rural labour. On such assumptions, the conclusion must necessarily be that accelerated population growth results in the appearance of food shortages, co-existent with a lack of employment opportunities.

Is it realistic to assume that the cultivators attempt to undertake the investments and can they succeed in doing so? Let us take the last question first. The answer to this question depends on one hand on the size and character of the additional investment needed, private as well as public, and on the other hand on the amount of work which the agriculturalists performed, before population growth began to accelerate.

With a given rate of population growth in a given territory the amount of investment per head is likely to become larger and larger the more densely populated the territory becomes, because the land

---

[1] Large multi-purpose schemes designed to provide irrigation facilities as a by-product of large-scale hydro-power production are exceptions, of course, to this statement.

improvements with lowest investment cost per unit of additional output are likely to be chosen before the less remunerative ones. Moreover, the increasing intensity of land use reduces the off-season leisure periods, with the result that the ability to carry an additional work burden becomes smaller and smaller, when the burden becomes larger. Since the size of the burden is dependent also on the rate of population growth, the conclusion is that the rate of population growth which a given rural community can sustain by its own efforts becomes smaller the more densely populated its territory becomes.

The capacity of work of the labour and peasant families set an upper limit to the process of adaptation by means of additional toil. When the stage is reached where all able-bodied members of the rural communities, males and females, young and old, are labouring from sunrise to sunset all the year, the community has reached the point where additional investment can be undertaken only if current work is reduced and *per capita* food consumption declines. The introduction of agricultural communes in China was no doubt an attempt to avoid a decline of *per capita* food production by pushing the performance of work to this point of maximum employment.[1]

INVESTMENT UNDER FAMILY FARMING

In the discussion of investment in tribal communities (chapter 10) it was stressed that not only the physical ability to shoulder an added investment burden, but also the incentives to do so must be taken into account. The same can be said of communities which have

---

[1] It is assumed here that a high level of rural employment obtains in China. This is in accordance with the results of the old inquiry by Lossing Buck (mentioned in chapter 5 and in note 1, page 53) and with the opinions of T. H. Shen (op. cit., pp. 115 ff.). This assumption of a high level of rural employment also tallies with more recent facts, viz. the failure of the Government to make the communes produce a sufficient amount of current output of food while the volume of investment and non-agricultural work done by the peasants was at the same time stepped up very considerably. On the face of it, this may appear to be flatly contradicted by the facts reported by Professor Dumont, *Révolution dans les campagnes chinoises* (Paris, 1957). René Dumont observed that, in many of the co-operative farms he visited in 1955–6, the average number of days per year reported to have been spent on collective work was very low. However, work-days spent on such activities as the collection and preparation of manure for the co-operative were not reckoned as collective work-days, since such manure had to be delivered in kind by the members (as mentioned by René Dumont, op. cit., p. 161). Likewise, all work on the peasants' private plots and with private animals was, of course, excluded. Moreover, the farms visited were not a representative sample, but had crop yields far above the regional averages. It is possible that they obtained these unusually high crop yields because they had excessive supplies of labour, and could apply labour-intensive practices to a still larger extent than farms with a more typical labour-land ratio.

passed the tribal stage. In other words, we must ask if the family solidarity in settled peasant communities is more likely to survive the change to a money economy than is tribal solidarity.

Professor Leibenstein's theory of economic-demographic growth is based upon the assumption that in a backward economy population growth will have only a very limited effect as an inducement to greater investment. He does not believe that additional investment would be undertaken in a backward economy just because the number of mouths to feed is increasing. In his opinion, investments will come about only when more purchasing power is anticipated, which in turn implies higher income.[1]

In my opinion, Leibenstein is paying too little attention to the fact that the motivations governing decisions about investment are different in communities with family enterprises from what they are in communities with large-scale enterprise utilizing mainly or exclusively wage labour. The son of a peasant or artisan is very closely tied to his family and has a strong personal interest in the family enterprise. Even under a money economy he is likely to stay at home and use the years when he is already an efficient worker, while not yet provided with a family of his own, to work in the family enterprise with work hours of a length depending on circumstances, including the need for investments which are meant to help himself to support his future family.

As long as the annual burden of work per man is so moderate in a given community that the young generation can do the investment necessary to support their own future families as off-season activity without reducing their participation in current agricultural work, investment need not become a limiting factor for agricultural production, even when the rate of growth of rural population is very considerable. Moreover, the young man need not do all the work, but can draw on other family members. It is well known that parents are willing to undergo considerable privation in order to provide a bride price for a son's marriage or a dowry for a daughter's wedding. It would be strange if they were less generous, when they have to labour in order to accommodate the new couple by land improvement.

In a cultivator family with a single son, who is approaching marrying age, it is likely that the son does a large share of the current work, while women and elder men in the main restrict their participation to periods of peak activity. In a family with two sons to settle it is likely that these between them share most of the heavy investment work necessary to create subsistence for two future families instead of one,

[1] H. Leibenstein, 'Population Growth and the Take-off Hypothesis', in W. W. Rostow (ed.), op. cit., pp. 179–80.

while the less able-bodied members of the family do more current work than those in smaller families. This method of enabling investment to be done resembles that of the feudal system, where the landlords used the peasants' sons to do the investment for their own future family households, while other members of the peasant communities had to work harder in their own holdings in order to pay the taxes in kind which were used to feed the workers doing the actual investment.

It follows from the analysis of land use in previous chapters, that a cultivator family's ability to create additional agricultural capital for the settling of a new and larger generation does not depend on whether or not it has access to uncultivated land. A peasant with two sons may improve his land and thus permit his sons to share the family land and have enough for each of them. In order to do so, they need not necessarily change to another cropping pattern and be dependent upon the existence of marketing facilities for special crops. The widespread idea that a family can subsist on a smaller area only if it can find a market for labour-intensive and high-yielding crops is based on the assumption that the system of land use does not change. But this is to forget that if the land is cropped more frequently than before, the area may be reduced without the introduction of new crops. For instance, two sons may share the land of their father by having an irrigated crop of wheat each year instead of a dry one every second year, or by having two transplanted crops of paddy each year instead of one broadcast one. The increase of population in Asia in this century has been accompanied by a reduction of the area of fallow and by a very substantial increase of the area which is irrigated and cropped more than once, but the cropping pattern did not change very much.

REAL WAGES AND EMPLOYMENT

The reasoning above takes no account of the fact that in virtually all peasant communities a share of the cultivators use hired labour for the cultivation of their land in addition to or instead of family labour. At least some of these cultivators would have other possibilities of arranging their children's future than by intensifying the pattern of land use in their own holdings. Production in holdings relying mainly on hired labour will become intensified only if the increase of population either causes an increase of food prices without a corresponding increase in money wages or results in lower money wages with unchanged food prices. If food prices remain unchanged despite the increase of population the holdings relying on hired labour lack the inducement to intensify production and there will tend to be a lack of employment opportunities for the increasing numbers in the labour families which can find employment in agriculture only by offering to work for lower money wages.[1]

Some economists deny the possibility of either of these processes of adaptation. They point to the very low real wages for agricultural work in most pre-industrial rural communities and assert that real wages cannot be reduced further without outright starvation for the wage labourers. The corollary is that balance must be restored by an increase in mortality and not by an expansion of agricultural production. This holds good only if it is true either that no significant increase in average employment per family can be obtained by the reduction of real wages, or that real wages decline to a level where earnings from additional employment could not even buy the additional food consumed by a working compared to a non-working person. I doubt that these assumptions are likely to be realistic in any underdeveloped country.

It was suggested in chapter 5 that an intensification of the pattern of land use, particularly when it goes together with the introduction of better water control, is likely to cause a fundamental change in the seasonal pattern of employment in agriculture. In such cases a reduction of real wages per man-hour may be more than offset by additional employment. Thus, at this stage of agricultural development, a decline of real wages per man-hour may go together with an increase of annual real incomes of the labour families.

But changes in the seasonal pattern of employment are not the only way in which labour families at this stage of agricultural development may get additional employment. When population increase makes it necessary to change to intensive land use, the share of total employment which falls on the landless labourers is likely to rise, and it may perhaps rise more than the share of landless in total agricultural population. In order to explain this point it is necessary to look at the structure of the rural labour market in densely populated pre-industrial economies.

In typical villages in such economies we have a small group of cultivators which uses hired labour only for the cultivation of their land and a larger group which uses some hired labour, mainly in the peak seasons, but mostly rely on family labour. The labourers who work for these groups also fall in two categories one of which consists of landless people, while the other group—sometimes much larger—consists of peasants who are themselves cultivators of small

[1] A downward pressure on agricultural wages may occur also for another reason. Peasants who used to rent part of their land to tenants may increasingly replace these tenants by family members, when their own families are growing in size. Members of the tenant families would thereby be pushed into the group of wage labourers.

plots of owned or rented land, but who in addition work as labourers for other cultivators, mainly in the peak seasons.

If real wages decline, either because food prices increase or because money wages decline, the landless labourers have no other choice than to reduce their leisure and that of their wives and children and to offer to work for very low wages in the off-season periods. Those labourers who have some land to cultivate are more likely to react by limiting their supply of wage labour and instead cultivating this land more intensively with family labour. Since they took wage labour mainly in the peak seasons, their limitation of the supply of wage labour may prevent a major decline of real wages in the peak seasons and there is thus put a floor below which the real incomes of the landless labourers cannot easily fall. There is often a very large discrepancy between rural wages in the peak season and in the off-season in pre-industrial communities.

The reduction of off-season real wages is an important incentive for the intensification of the pattern of land use in holdings relying on hired labour, since the additional employment that goes with more intensive land use falls largely in the off-seasons, as previously explained.

The group of landless labourers may get added employment not only because of more off-season work and perhaps less competition from labourers with land of their own. They may also get additional employment because the low real wages in the off-seasons induce some cultivators who hitherto used hired labour in the peak seasons to have also their off-season work, or part of it, done by labourers. In rural communities where population pressure reduces off-season real wages to very low levels and pushes up rents, land-owning peasants will seize the opportunity of their stronger position as employers (and perhaps also as leasers of land) and begin to use hired labour for operations which were formerly done by family labour. We get a process where seasonal unemployment in the village is reduced but where at the same time the better-off cultivator families limit family labour to some help to the hired labourers in the peak season.

The result of these changes is a revolution in the pattern of employment of the landless labourers. From having long idle periods each year, they get full or nearly full employment all the year, while the remaining seasonal underemployment in the village becomes concentrated on the well-to-do. There seem to be little reason to assume that the labour families are reduced to starvation by this process; they probably eat better than when they were underemployed labourers with long idle periods. If they did not do so, they might not be able to perform hard work all the year. But the improvement in their overall consumption standard, if there is one, is out of proportion to the added toil which all able-bodied members of the labour families must endure. We must keep in mind this increasing inequality in the distribution of toil and leisure in densely populated pre-industrial villages, if we wish to understand the logic of popular land reform movements of the Chinese type, under which people risked execution on the main evidence of having hands unmarked by work.

The changes which take place in the pattern of employment and the possibilities of divergent trends of peak-season and off-season wages imply that no close correlation can be expected to exist between changes in the real wage of the marginal hour in agriculture (defined as the off-season wage) and in the standard of living of the agricultural labour families. The former may decline considerably, while the latter remains constant or increases.

But even if annual real incomes of the labour families were to decline, the result is not necessarily starvation, because food consumption may change to cheaper types of food, which were not produced or were little consumed even by the poorest, as long as population was smaller. There is evidence from densely populated countries in Asia and elsewhere that agricultural labourers and members of other low income groups change their consumption from the more expensive cereals like wheat and rice to the types of cereals which can grow on poor land and to high-yielding root crops like tapioca and potatoes when population becomes more dense and food prices increase or wages decline.[1]

The trends in Asian and in western European agriculture in the last century are so strikingly divergent that there is a danger of overlooking the similarities in development in earlier times. During the century of rapid population growth following the European agricultural revolution, both agricultural labourers and small peasants had to work much harder in agriculture and to rely to an increasing extent on help from family members for the tasks of taking care of livestock and producing labour-intensive crops both for fodder and for human consumption. Some of these crops, such as turnips and potatoes, required hard manual work in periods which had previously been periods of leisure, and this work was to a large extent performed by members of the labour families and those of the small peasants who had to hire out their labour. The average number of hours

---

[1] 'Sweet potato growing has extended in many provinces in the middle of the eighteenth century, a circumstance believed to be related to the great increase in the Chinese population during the period of stable government and peaceful conditions.' T. H. Shen, op. cit., p. 212. A similar switch of consumption from rice to other crops appears to have taken place in Japan in the nineteenth century. Tobata Seiichi, *An Introduction to the Agriculture of Japan* (Tokyo, 1958), p. 5, and Kazushi Ohkawa *et al.*, *The Growth of the Japanese Economy* (Tokyo, 1957), p. 51. Likewise, cassava has been gaining ground in Java in recent decades.

worked per year by a family of agricultural labourers and small peasants must have increased tremendously in the period from the agricultural revolution to the time when agricultural machinery became widespread.

The annual real incomes of the labourers and small peasants in western Europe probably improved little, if at all, in this period. It seems that rural consumption patterns changed from livestock products and cereals to increasing reliance on pork and potatoes, which were considered as inferior foods.[1]

FOOD PRICES AND TAXATION OF AGRICULTURE

The labour and peasant families' capacity for work sets the limit to the process of adaptation by increasing toil for the agricultural population, as already mentioned. The more this limit is approached, the larger is the share of the burden of added food production that falls on the urban population and, in extreme cases, the share of total population engaged in non-agricultural occupations may have to be reduced in order to speed up food production. Apart from economies of the Chinese type, the mechanism by which the burden of population increase is shifted from the rural to the urban population is usually improving terms of trade for agriculture in relation to the non-agricultural sectors.

Such a development of the sectoral terms of trade has been seen in Japan, where an already dense population was rapidly increasing until fairly recently. The increasing density of population raised prices of basic food to a level of world record after the end of the Second World War, while prices of industrial products were cheap compared with those of other countries. The result was to force both the agricultural and the non-agricultural population to work very hard, while using a large share of their incomes for basic food, and to encourage agriculturalists to use labour-intensive practices and to apply much industrial input in agriculture.

The Japanese government promoted a high labour input per person in agriculture by a policy of high food prices combined with a relatively high taxation of agriculture.[2] The high taxes forced the

---

[1] The decline of real wages in western European agriculture between the middle of the eighteenth and the middle of the nineteenth century is described in B. H. Slicher van Bath, op. cit., pp. 225–7; the change to cheaper food is mentioned, ibid., pp. 237 and 264–70. See also F. K. Riemann, *Ackerbau und Viehhaltung im vorindustriellen Deutschland* (Kitzingen-Main, 1953), pp. 126–31.

[2] The land tax accounted for 78 per cent of ordinary revenue (the bulk of total revenue) from 1868 to 1881, and although the figures tended to fall after that it still stood at 50 per cent in 1890. High as the rate of land tax was, however, it did not represent an increase over the Tokugawa period. Already at the end

land-owning peasants both to use the land intensively and to take part in manual work in spite of the high prices. It is interesting to compare this policy with that of India, where both price policy and tax policy are strikingly different from those of Japan.

Independent India is continuing with the policy of low food prices and low agricultural taxes, which had become customary in the colonial period. Prices of basic food at the farm gate are kept low by means of food imports, and land taxes and water rates together account for less than 2 per cent of the value of agricultural output.[1] The low prices give little incentive to intensive land use,[2] and the low taxes permit the land-owning peasants to enjoy relatively much leisure and a level of consumption, which, although low by the standard of many other countries in Asia, are considerably higher than that of the agricultural labourers.

With insufficient price encouragement to intensive land use, expansion of output in Indian agriculture becomes dependent on government investment and government subsidies, and since taxation of agriculture is low this places a heavy burden on the non-agricultural sectors.[3] Under these circumstances, the rapid growth of the Indian population must become a serious deterrent to development of the non-agricultural sectors, but it is possible to argue that these difficulties ought to be ascribed not so much to the fact of rapid population growth as such, but more to an agricultural policy which allows the landowners to evade their fair share of the economic burden of population increase.

---

of that period the take from agriculture by the warrior class was immense, and the Meiji Government merely redirected it into new channels. Modernization was achieved, therefore, without reducing rural living standards or even taking the increase in productivity that occurred. Thomas C. Smith, op. cit., p. 211.

[1] According to tables in 'Studies of the Economics of Farm Management', op. cit.

[2] See note 1, page 69.

[3] In an essay on economic policy in Ceylon, Professor Hicks suggested a few years ago that in order to provide incentive for more intensive cultivation of the land a universal tax on land should be levied, even if it would have to be accompanied by a further increase of the already high support price for paddy. See J. R. Hicks, *Essays in World Economics* (Oxford, 1959), p. 203.

CHAPTER 13

THE USE OF INDUSTRIAL INPUT IN PRIMITIVE AGRICULTURE

In discussions about the use of industrial input in primitive agriculture some economists draw a sharp line of distinction between labour-saving and land-saving kinds of input. In the view of these authors, labour-saving inputs are inappropriate in underdeveloped economies in periods of rapid growth of population, except for countries with much uncultivated land where such inputs might help to raise both total output and output per active in agriculture. In countries with little or no uncultivated land suitable for cultivation, only land-saving inputs such as industrial fertilizer and other chemicals should be used, according to this view, since they would raise not only output per active in agriculture but also total output, while the use of labour-saving inputs in such cases would add little or nothing to total output and might displace agricultural labour beyond the possibility of absorption in the urban sector. It is this fear of creating unemployment and underemployment in agriculture which lies behind the wish to distinguish between labour-saving and land-saving inputs.

How relevant in this distinction between labour-saving and land-saving inputs? It is relevant, it seems, only if and when it is permissible to disregard the possibility of an intensification of the forms of land use. In other words, it is relevant if agricultural development is conceived as consisting either in the bringing under cultivation of virgin land or in the improvement of yields per crop hectare by the application of additional units of labour and capital. But if, besides these possibilities, we allow for the use of industrial input as a help in the transition to more frequent cropping, then it becomes clear that the reasoning just referred to misses a very important point and that the conclusions usually drawn from it may well be misleading.

Mrs Joan Robinson has suggested that technical progress and capital accumulation because they originated in sparsely populated America have an inherently land-using bias, so that output per unit

112

of labour increases at a more rapid rate than the output per unit of land when modern agricultural techniques are introduced.[1] This is no doubt true if the input of labour and capital for a single crop in a given field is considered. The percentage increase in yields that can be obtained by chemical inputs is small compared to the percentage decline in input of labour that can be gained by the use of mechanized equipment in replacement of hoes or animal-drawn ploughs. But the conclusion is less obvious if the perspective is changed and we take into account that both mechanized equipment and chemical inputs can be used to allow more frequent cropping of the land.

In such a perspective, when the change-over from traditional agricultural methods to the use of industrial input is seen, not in the narrow framework of the individual field, but in the broader one of the whole pattern of land use in a given region, then it can be said of mechanized equipment as well as of chemical inputs that they may be either land-saving or labour-saving, depending upon the circumstances. Both mechanized equipment and chemical inputs are likely to be used as land-saving devices in cases where population increase and attractive prices stimulate to more intensive use of land, and as a labour-saving device in cases when a more intensive use of land appears to be pointless owing to stagnant demand or competition from food imports or for other reasons.

Let us first consider a country with constant population. The needed increase in total output of food would be that required to cope with the increase in *per capita* incomes and there would be little need to change the pattern of land use substantially. If there were any incentive to use industrial input in agriculture, this would primarily be as a means to release labour from agriculture, but this might be done *either* by the introduction of mechanized equipment in replacement of human labour, *or* by the substitution of chemical fertilizers for labour-intensive methods of fertilization, *or* by the use of chemical fertilizers as a means to concentrate production on the best land, while labour was saved by giving up the cultivation of poor-quality land. In the latter case, land utilization would become more intensive on the best land and less intensive on the poorest, but with little change in the average intensity of utilization of the land.

Let us now turn to a country with rapidly rising population and no possibility of feeding the additional inhabitants by means of food imports. If there would be any possibility of applying industrial input in agriculture, the incentive would be to use it as a means to obtain a major shift in the pattern of land utilization, and also in this case the aim could be obtained either by mechanized or by chemical inputs,

---

[1] Joan Robinson, *The Accumulation of Capital* (London, 1956), pp. 321 and 323–4.

or—more likely—by a combination of both. Chemical fertilizers would be used, not to replace but to supplement other means of fertilization, thus allowing still more frequent cropping; mechanized power would be used to provide water where this was impossible or very difficult to do by traditional methods; and tractors would first of all be used for contour ploughing and similar land improvements, which would make possible a more efficient use of the land. When mechanized equipment is used for such purposes, far from superseding labour it helps to increase employment opportunities.

In most countries there are some districts which can be irrigated only at exorbitant cost, if at all. If rapid population growth makes it impossible to forgo the output of such dry lands, the choice may be between permanent agrarian underemployment in that region or a partial depopulation made possible by mechanization of all peak operations. If the redundant agricultural population is transferred to less irregular employment in regions better suited for irrigated, multi-crop agriculture, the partial tractorization in the dry and poor agricultural region may turn out to have added both to total output and to total agricultural employment.

When the possibilities of intensification of land use by means of industrial input are taken into account, the full productive potentiality of modern agricultural methods becomes apparent. To gauge the full productive potentiality of chemical fertilizer one must remember not only the fruits it bears in the shape of increased yields per crop hectare, but also its effect in replacing fallow and allowing annual cropping or multiple cropping in cases where more extensive systems of land use would otherwise have been called for. To gauge the full productive potentialities of the agricultural tractor—particularly in very densely populated regions—one must remember not only the land improvements which can be made by means of it, but also its land-saving effects in making pastures for draught animals superfluous, saving crops which would otherwise be lost, and facilitating multiple cropping.

The savings of land which can be obtained by replacing the draught animals by tractors (and their manure by chemical fertilizer) require no further comment. It is of course particularly large in regions where custom or religious belief prevent any other use of the draught animals. The use of the tractor for saving crops either because sowing can be done in time or because harvesting can be done quickly is not less obvious.[1] But the largest advantage of tractorization in very

---

[1] Tractors were introduced in East Pakistan, a region of extreme density of population, in order to make it possible to plough the land quickly after the rains and thus improve crop yields. J. R. Andrus, *The Economy of Pakistan* (Stanford, 1958), p. 39.

densely populated regions seems to be the possibility of performing the peak operations so quickly as to make room for an additional crop within a limited growing season. Japan which has reached a high degree of mechanization is now able, despite a relatively long cold season, to reap three crops annually in a large part of its cultivated area.

CHAPTER 14

SOME PERSPECTIVES AND
IMPLICATIONS

Agriculture in Europe and the United States has undergone a radical transformation in the last century. Scientific methods of cultivation have been introduced and mechanized equipment and other industrial products have become widely used.

On the background of this technical revolution of agricultural procedures in the already developed world, agrarian change in underdeveloped countries may seem trivial, and it is understandable that many economists should presume that in countries where agriculture has not yet reached the stage of scientific and industrial methods it is stagnant and traditional, almost by definition.

The preceding chapters should have shown that this view is unwarranted, and that in the supposedly immutable communities of primitive agriculture profound changes are in fact occurring.

Students of economic history have not failed to describe the successive changes within primitive agricultural systems, but this has largely passed unnoticed by economists. They tended to regard the existing methods of cultivation and systems of land use as permanent features of a given locality, reflecting its particular natural conditions, rather than as phases in a process of economic development. In accordance with this view, the causal explanation of differences in cultivation systems was supposed to be a matter for geographers to consider; and these would naturally be inclined to explain differences in agricultural methods in terms of climatic conditions, type of soil and other natural factors which were believed to remain uninfluenced by changes in the size of population. It is in the logic of this approach to expect that major increases of agricultural population within a given area must result in the emergence of a labour surplus on the land and a consequent pressure for migration to other regions or to urban areas.

Our investigation in the preceding pages lends no support to this conception of an agrarian surplus population emerging as the result of population growth. We have found that it is unrealistic to regard agricultural cultivation systems as adaptations to different natural conditions, and that cultivation systems can be more plausibly explained as the result of differences in population density: As long as the population of a given area is very sparse, food can be produced with little input of labour per unit of output and with virtually no capital investment, since a very long fallow period helps to preserve soil fertility. As the density of population in the area increases, the fertility of the soil can no longer be preserved by means of long fallow and it becomes necessary to introduce other systems which require a much larger agricultural labour force. By the gradual change from systems where each cultivated plot is matched by twenty similar plots under fallow to systems where no fallow is necessary, the population within a given area can double several times without having to face either starvation or lack of employment opportunities in agriculture.

Some economic historians, noting the process of gradual shortening of fallow with accompanying changes in methods in many rural communities, made the observation that these changes occurred in periods of increasing population. The mere observation of this relationship leaves us with the further question of whether the increase in population is the effect or the cause of the agrarian changes.

The empirical study of the historical sequence is not very helpful in answering this question. Changes in patterns of land utilization and in agricultural methods usually occur gradually over long periods, and the same is most often true of demographic changes. Therefore, it is often difficult or impossible to determine through historical research whether the demographic change was the cause or the effect of the changes in agricultural methods. In the absence of a clear answer from historical sources, many historians have been inclined to presume a line of causation conforming to Malthusian theory, with the agrarian change as the cause and the long-term demographic trend as the effect.

Chapters 3 and 4 in the present study attempt to approach from another angle this important question of what is cause and what is effect. The method is the indirect one of comparing labour costs per unit of output in the main systems of primitive agriculture. The conclusion drawn from this comparison was that the complex changes which are taking place when primitive communities change over to a system of shorter fallow are more likely to raise labour costs per unit of output than to reduce them. Therefore, it seems implausible to explain upwards changes in rates of population growth as a result of this type of agrarian change. It is more sensible to regard the process of agricultural change in primitive communities as an adaptation to gradually increasing population densities, brought about by changes in the rates of natural population growth or by immigration.

According to the explanation offered here, population increase leads to the adoption of more intensive systems of agriculture in primitive communities and an increase of total agricultural output. This process, however, can hardly be described as economic growth in the generally accepted sense of this term, since the proximate effect upon output per man-hour is to lower it. But sustained growth of total population and of total output in a given territory has secondary effects which—at least in some cases—can set off a genuine process of economic growth, with rising output per man-hour, first in non-agricultural activities and later in agriculture. Such secondary effects come about through two different mechanisms. On the one hand, the intensification of agriculture may compel cultivators and agricultural labourers to work harder and more regularly. This can produce changes in work habits which help to raise overall productivity. On the other hand, the increasing population density facilitates the division of labour and the spread of communications and education. The important corollary of this is that primitive communities with sustained population growth have a better chance to get into a process of genuine economic development than primitive communities with stagnant or declining population, provided of course, that the necessary agricultural investments are undertaken. This condition may not be fulfilled in densely peopled communities if rates of population growth are high.

According to the theory propounded above, a period of sustained population growth would first have the effect of lowering output per man-hour in agriculture, but in the long run the effect might be to raise labour productivity in other activities and eventually to raise output per man-hour also in agriculture. In a development pattern of this kind, there is likely to be an intermediary stage where labour productivity in agriculture is declining while that of other activities is increasing. This period is likely to be one of considerable political and social tension, because people in rural areas, instead of voluntarily accepting the harder toil of a more intensive agriculture, will seek to obtain more remunerative and less arduous work in non-agricultural occupations. In such periods, large-scale migrations to urban areas are likely to take place and to result in hardening competition in urban labour markets. The flight from the land may reach such proportions that it precludes the necessary expansion of food production in the villages, with the result that the town population must carry the double burden of lacking employment opportunities and high food prices. Difficulties of this type have occurred in most developing countries in the past, and they have been dealt with in very different ways: some European countries went as far as to re-introduce rural serfdom in order to curb the drift of rural youth to the towns; others tried to counteract internal migration by legal restrictions, or to introduce agrarian reform as an incentive for people to remain in the rural areas.

In cases where the migrations from village to town at this stage of development are allowed to continue without restraint, the ensuing relative rise of food prices may provide the needed incentive for an intensification of agriculture and be followed by a rise of rural money wages which helps to keep migration within bounds.

An alternative to the acceptance of rising food prices is to allow the importation of food. Increased food imports at this stage of develop-ment is a means to avoid the political and social trouble in the urban areas which would be likely to follow rising prices of food in terms of urban wages. However, if the import of food contributes to prevent or retard the intensification of domestic agriculture, the inflow of rural labour to the towns may continue. The result may be a slack labour market in urban and rural areas, particularly in cases where the need to finance the food imports leads to measures which reduce employment opportunities in the urban areas.

In the past century, the pressure of population growth was miti-gated in many underdeveloped countries by the possibility of sus-tained expansion of the production of tropical crops for exports. The rapid growth of both population and *per capita* incomes in many countries in the temperate zones created expanding markets for such crops at prices which were so high that cultivators, by changing over from food production for domestic consumption to production of export crops, could earn a subsistence wage or income with a smaller input of labour than would be required to obtain the same income by the production of food crops in intensive systems of agriculture. Therefore, increasing numbers of the rising populations in many underdeveloped countries took to the cultivation of export crops.

The type of development just described is characterized by a sharp contrast between the sector producing for exports and the sector which continues to produce food for subsistence. The rising numbers in the export sector are consuming mainly food and non-agricultural goods imported from other areas. The stagnant or gradually declining numbers in the subsistence sector continue to produce their own food by long-fallow systems, have little division of labour and contribute little to the growth of urbanization, which is limited to one or a few centres of foreign trade.

World markets for tropical export crops are no longer expanding so quickly that they can provide sufficient outlet for the more and more rapidly growing rural populations in the tropical countries. These are faced with the choice between harder work in more intensive food production, or migration to urban areas. They seem in most cases to choose the latter solution in so great numbers that urban labour markets become oversupplied with unskilled labour, while the labour supply in rural areas is insufficient to allow the needed shift from long fallow to more intensive agriculture. It thus seems that now, as in the past, there is a choice between increasing food prices, food imports or direct government intervention, in one form or the other, against migrations from the countryside.

It might be objected that the recent revolution of agricultural techniques has changed the situation fundamentally in this respect and that an additional solution is now available, namely to modernize and increase food production by means of industrial input, mechanized equipment as well as chemical fertilizers. But in primitive rural communities in countries where food is cheap in terms of prices of industrial goods there appears to be little incentive to use industrial inputs in agriculture. Thus the possibility of stepping up agricultural output by the introduction of modern industrial inputs cannot be realized unless a rise in agricultural prices relative to those of industrial goods is allowed to take place.

This leads on to the final question: What are the implications of the present study for the possibilities of promoting economic growth in the underdeveloped parts of the world? Can history teach us anything for the future, or has it become irrelevant under modern conditions with the possibility of using scientific methods and industrial products in the agriculture of underdeveloped countries?

It is clear that this question cannot be answered by a reference to the fact that output per man-hour in agriculture increases by leaps and bounds when industrial methods are introduced in rural communities in already industrialized countries. Similar changes raise output per man-hour much less when introduced in underdeveloped countries where rural skills and rural communications remain at primitive levels. The modest increases in output per man-hour which can be obtained by the use of industrial products or scientific methods in such communities may not be sufficient to pay for the very scarce resources of skilled labour and foreign exchange which they absorb. It seems somewhat unrealistic, therefore, to assume that a revolution of agricultural techniques by means of modern industrial and scientific methods will take place in the near future in countries which have not yet reached the stage of urban industrialization. It is not very likely, in other words, that we shall see a reversion of the traditional sequence, in which the urban sector tends to adopt modern methods a relatively long time before the agricultural sector undergoes a corresponding transformation. Past experience may therefore still **have** some relevance for the planning of agricultural growth in the underdeveloped world.

INDEX